The Saturn Difference

The Saturn Difference

*Creating Customer Loyalty
in Your Company*

Vicki Lenz

John Wiley & Sons, Inc.
New York • Chichester • Weinheim • Brisbane • Singapore • Toronto

This book is printed on acid-free paper. ∞

Published by John Wiley & Sons, Inc.
Published simultaneously in Canada.

This publication is designed to provide accurate and authoritative information in regard to the subject matter covered. It is sold with the understanding that the publisher is not engaged in rendering legal, accounting, or other professional services. If legal advice or other expert assistance is required, the services of a competent professional person should be sought.

Library of Congress Cataloging-in-Publication Data:
Lenz, Vicki.
    The Saturn difference : creating customer loyalty in your company / Vicki Lenz.
      p.   cm.
    Includes index.
    ISBN 0-471-31449-8 (alk. paper)
    1. Consumer satisfaction. 2. Customer relations. I. Title.
HF5415.5.L46   1999
658.8'12—dc21   98-38406
                                      CIP

Printed in the United States of America.
10 9 8 7 6 5 4 3 2 1

To enthusiastic Saturn team members
and customers everywhere—thanks
for making this story possible!

Contents

Preface

IF YOU'RE THINKING THAT THIS BOOK WAS SATURN'S IDEA, THE answer is definitely NO. And, no, I was not under contract or employed by Saturn Corporation, General Motors, or any advertising agency to write this book. Let me share with you the story behind it.

I was first exposed to Saturn several years ago when a friend purchased a shiny black Saturn coupe. She was so enthusiastic that you would have thought Saturn was paying her to act that way. (The company wasn't, but later the local retailer did invite her to appear in commercials and newspaper advertisements.) Then, in another book, I wrote about Saturn's 1994 Homecoming event as a means for showing customer appreciation and creating generations of customers. Later, as I began speaking to business audiences, I mentioned the Homecoming—and interesting things happened. Enthusiastic people—loyal Saturn customers—approached me, anxious to share their stories. Stories about why Saturn is different. Stories not so much about the car; rather, stories about the wonderful way they were treated as customers before, during, and after they purchased one. The more I heard, and the more I learned about Saturn, the more I became convinced that the whole Saturn customer experience and way of doing business were really something special. In fact, so much customer enthusiasm rubbed off on me that, when it came time for me to buy a new car, I decided to buy a Saturn for myself!

The folks at the facility where I purchased my car weren't aware that I would be writing this book, so I didn't get preferential treatment. Well, that's really not correct to say, since Saturn's standard practice is that *every* customer gets preferential treatment. I'm proud to say that as a Saturn customer, I have been treated just as all other Saturn customers are treated: ROYALLY. One sales manager told me about a prospective customer informing her that since he would be buying two cars, he expected "special treatment." She gladly informed him that "You're in luck, because *all* of our customers get special treatment!"

Most of us can relate to buying a car. Usually, we rate a car-buying experience right up there with an IRS audit, or going to the dentist. What I found is that people outside "the Saturn family" just don't know the story, or understand what all the hoopla is about. Throughout my 20-plus-years in sales, marketing, and consulting, I've also found that business people learn best from the positive examples set by other companies. And that customers can teach you a lot. The result is this book, which is my way of observing and sharing the best of what works.

What began with comments from a handful of Saturn customers grew to include my interviews with hundreds of happy, enthusiastic Saturn customers. Then, helpful Saturn folks gladly filled in with information and shared a few of their own stories. Added to that were research and my own observations as a Saturn customer—and as a customer who appreciates being treated right.

Which brings me to the other side of the story—how all of us are treated as customers on a daily basis. Admit it, wouldn't you like all of *your* experiences as a customer to be pleasant experiences? Unfortunately, that is rarely the case. My hope is that reading about Saturn will encourage other businesses to become more customer-focused—and make customer experiences nicer for all of us!

So, here's the story. At times, the question "Is this for real?" will enter your mind. It entered mine more than once as I interviewed customers and conducted research. Rest assured that the whole story *is* for real. I hope you enjoy it, learn from it, and apply it to your business so that you're wildly successful, and your customers are loyal!

About Saturn
and Customer
Loyalty

Introduction

DO YOU KNOW A SATURN CAR OWNER? CHANCES ARE THAT IF YOU ask a roomful of a hundred people, you'll find two or three Saturn customers. And do you know what happens when they're asked to share their experiences as Saturn customers? They get a smile on their faces . . . their eyes light up . . . and they can't wait to tell everyone why they are LOYAL customers!

These loyal, enthusiastic customers deluge Saturn with complimentary letters, e-mail, cards, posters, pictures, and notes of thanks. They write poems and sing songs about Saturn. They set up web sites about Saturn on the Internet. When was the last time you felt that way about a company with which you do business? Or when did your customers last feel that way about *your* business? Never? Maybe it's like the back of the Saturn CarClub T-shirt that reads, "If you don't own one, you probably wouldn't understand."

Why Saturn as the Role Model?

Saturn rightly refers to itself as "a different kind of company." Saturn leaders and team members didn't intend to reinvent customer loyalty. Nor do they lay claim to the distinction. In fact, what you normally hear around Saturn is "customer enthusiasm," not customer loyalty. Enthusiasm leads to loyalty. The way I see it, in less than one decade of existence, Saturn has emerged as THE role model for customer loyalty. Sure, there are plenty of other companies with lots of loyal customers, that set great examples. But how many companies purposely target "customer enthusiasm" in their mission statement?

Saturn, the young small-car unit (a wholly owned subsidiary) of General Motors Corporation, successfully meets the challenge of providing high levels of product, sales, and service satisfaction, according to results from J.D. Power and Associates studies. In fact, the Saturn ownership experience is now considered by many in the automotive world to be the standard by which customer satisfaction is measured. Saturn is the perennial leader in the J.D. Power and Associates annual Sales Satisfaction Index, and the latest Customer Satisfaction Index put Saturn in seventh place (the top six were all luxury cars). One J.D. Power official observed that the top-ranking companies seem to have developed a corporate culture that stresses keeping the customer happy long after the car is sold.

Saturn has received numerous awards over the years, from being named by *Popular Science* magazine as one of "The Year's 100 Greatest Achievements in Science and Technology," to receiving *Home Mechanix* magazine's "Easy Maintenance of the Year Award." Saturn has received awards for design, engineering, driver's choice, and technology. Congratulations were offered to Saturn in 1998 on the selection of six out of seven of its vehicles to the IntelliChoice list of "Best Overall Values of the Year." IntelliChoice is one of the most respected automotive information providers in the United States, and publisher of the award-winning *The Complete Car Cost Guide*. For six years in a row a Saturn sedan has won an IntelliChoice "Best Overall Value," and for five consecutive years the SL Series won the "Best Overall

Value" in its class. You can read about even more awards in Chapter 2.

In an industry where the average customer loyalty rate hovers at around 44 percent, Saturn excels at close to 60 percent. Saturn's customer loyalty rate is now higher than those of its chief foreign competitors—Toyota and Honda. Pretty darn good for an auto manufacturer that has had only three products (coupe, sedan, and wagon) and eight short years to develop repeat-purchasing customers. Since Saturn plans on being around in 100-plus years from now, long-term customers are important. Tune in as Don Hudler, president and chairman of Saturn Corporation, describes how customer loyalty contributes to Saturn's success:

> Customer loyalty is Saturn's foundation as a 100-plus year car company. A long-term relationship with the people who buy our car becomes important as we grow our brand and offer more products. Saturn's industry-leading loyalty gives us an advantage in a fickle car market. We want people to be enthusiastic with their current Saturn and return to us when [they need] another car. There is no stronger or [more] credible voice in the market about the Saturn Difference—loyal and enthusiastic customers become advocates for our product and bring new buyers to our "family."

And after talking with hundreds of members of the Saturn family (customers), I can sum everything up in one word: WOW! It's no wonder that close to 13,000 enthusiastic and loyal Saturn customers have formed their own car clubs across the country. Or that 44,000 owners and their families made the trip to Spring Hill, Tennessee, in 1994 for a "Homecoming"—just to enjoy a barbecue, visit the factory where their cars were made, and meet the people who made them.

Now, I'm not suggesting that you become another Saturn Corporation. My point is this: Learn from what has worked for Saturn and Saturn customers.

Ten Reasons to Create Customer Loyalty

1. Loyal customers will spend more with you. Profit margins will increase.

2. Loyal customers tend to understand and appreciate value, and are less likely to price-shop.

3. Loyal customers mean repeat, long-term business (and those dollars add up!).

4. Loyal customers serve as a fantastic marketing force, providing the best kind of advertising available: word-of-mouth.

5. Loyal customers stick with you through difficult times.

6. Loyal customers can deliver a blow to your competition, because if customers are loyal to you, your competition isn't getting their business!

7. Loyal customers are your cheerleaders, and will go to bat for you.

8. Loyal customers tend to tell you what they like and dislike (yes, this is good—you want to know both).

9. Creating an atmosphere of customer loyalty within your company can be a great recruiting tool, and help the right employees come to you. Customer loyalty can boost employee morale and reduce turnover.

10. It just plain feels good when you treat people right, which is a key ingredient for creating loyal customers.

Warning: Customer Satisfaction Is NOT the Same as Customer Loyalty!

Customer satisfaction programs are weapons that many companies use in fighting the battles in today's marketplace. That's a step in the right direction, but the truth is that customer satisfaction does not necessarily translate into customer loyalty. Research has shown that 60 to 70 percent of customers who defect to the competition responded to a survey that they were "satisfied" or "very satisfied" with their previous supplier!

It's not enough to meet our customers' expectations; we must exceed them.

Don Hudler, Saturn president
From a banner hanging in Saturn's new Welcome Center

The difference between satisfaction and loyalty is that satisfaction is typically concerned only with the initial buying experience, the "how you get it" part, while loyalty is the product of building relationships for the long term. The secret, if there is one, is to think of customers in terms of relationships, not transactions. A consistent theme of quality, value, and service runs through the Saturn ownership experience, creating higher loyalty rates and unparalleled levels of customer enthusiasm.

What You'll Find in This Book

Although you will find some pretty interesting stuff here about Saturn cars, this book is not really about the car. It *is* about all the things combined that customers like, and that are important in creating customer loyalty. And it is about how Saturn has reinvented—and continues to create—the atmosphere necessary for customer loyalty. This is not theory, and it is not complicated. In fact, simplicity is what makes this loyalty style attractive AND what makes it work.

The Saturn Difference: Creating Customer Loyalty in Your Company, featuring the Saturn style of business as the role model, is a guide for turning one-time customers into repeat-purchasing loyal customers. Examples from various other businesses and companies are included as well. "The voice of the customer" is evident throughout the book, in the form of quotes that help emphasize points and tell stories. (Yes, they are real quotes from real Saturn customers.) Plus, you'll be treated to plenty of "What You Can Do" suggestions, along with a summarized "Key Point" at the end of each chapter.

Part One (Chapters 1 through 4) presents a brief history of Saturn Corporation, then covers the starting point and necessary basics for creating customer loyalty. Here you'll find Saturn's mission statement, philosophy, and values. And if you need some convincing that creating customer loyalty is a worthwhile thing to do, you'll discover the answers to your "What's in it for me?" question.

Part Two (Chapters 5 through 10) presents my breakdown of the ideal sales process—before, during, and after the purchase. These chapters tell how a customer's experience *should be*—for any product or service, from any size or type of business. They tell how Saturn does it, what customers think about it, and suggest how you can do it. It's my belief that it's easier to remember a process when it's broken down into six steps, so that's why the six chapters appear as:

1. Create Interest

2. Help Customers Feel Welcome

3. Make the Buying Process Easy

4. Communicate AFTER the Sale

5. Solve Problems

6. Keep Customers Coming Back

Part Three contains the rest of the story. In Chapter 11, you'll get more of the inside scoop on Saturn, through a question and answer session with Joe Kennedy, Saturn's vice president of sales, service, and marketing. Chapter 12 finishes with encouragement to "Saturnize" your company, using an easy-to-remember acronym.

I know that many of you are thinking, "This is a book about a car company, but my business is not the same." The fact is that whatever your business, you need customers to survive. Keeping customers for the longterm is immensely valuable, as you'll see in Chapter 3. Business people in positions ranging from receptionist to customer service rep, from sales rep to manager, and from small business owner to CEO, will find something useful in this book. *Any* business concerned about increasing sales and growth can relate to the observations and helpful analyses. You will find points of value that will benefit you directly if you will apply them.

So, rather than reinvent the wheel all over again, why not learn what works FOR customers . . . FROM customers, and from the company that has paved the road to serve as the model for customer loyalty!

A Brief History of Saturn

A Different Kind of Company.

A Different Kind of Car.

The Name

Many people may think that Saturn was named after the planet. Even the company logo appears to be the ringed planet Saturn. However, it was a different kind of celestial inspiration that gave the company its name. Saturn's goal was to design an American vehicle that could beat the Japanese in the small-car race. Several decades earlier, the United States had been in a similar race with another country: the space race with the USSR. In the end, NASA's Saturn booster rockets carried Americans to the moon, winning the race. Phil Garcia, chief designer in the advanced studio at the GM design center, is credited with selecting Saturn as the code name for GM's small-car project—the one that would boost GM to the head of the small-car class.

The Beginnings

The early 1980s constituted one of the most difficult periods in the history of the American auto industry. Each of the Big

Three automobile companies had lost market share and suffered major reductions in employment. Critics claimed that the Japanese were ruling the small-car segment. In July 1982, General Motors funded an engineering study to design a new product that could better compete with Japanese manufacturers. Saturn was thus born as a code name for the innovative project. GM needed Saturn to win back those customers who had given up on American small cars—a task deemed impossible by many auto analysts.

In late 1983, then-GM Chairman Roger B. Smith and President F. James McDonald jointly announced the Saturn project to the world, describing it as "the key to GM's long-term competitiveness, survival, and success as a domestic producer." They went on to predict that "1985, we strongly believe, will be the Year of the Saturn—the year when we affirm that American ingenuity, American technology, and American productivity can once again be the model and the inspiration for the rest of the world."[1]

The task of reviewing new relationships and approaches for the Saturn operation was given to Donald F. Ephlin, vice president and director of the United Auto Workers' General Motors Department, and Alfred A. Warren Jr., vice president of GM's Industrial Relations staff. Ephlin and Warren quickly realized that the project was bigger than what a handful of people could tackle, so they put together a larger group. In February 1984, the "Group of 99" came together. (You read that right! Can you imagine a committee of 99 people accomplishing anything?) It was made up of United Auto Worker (UAW) members, GM managers, and staff personnel from 55 plants in 17 GM divisions, and 14 of 16 UAW regions.

The Group of 99 was given basically three things to start with:

1. Instructions to use a "clean-sheet-of-paper approach."

2. The Mission: *Explore ways to integrate people and technology to manufacture small cars in the United States.*

3. The Philosophy: *We believe that all people want to be involved in decisions that affect them, care about their jobs, take pride in their accomplishments, and want to share in the success of their efforts.*

Armed with these instructions, the group organized into teams, then set out to study different companies and processes around the globe. They studied the best of the best in terms of quality, service, or cost leaders in their respective industries. In two months, the teams visited 49 GM plants and 60 benchmark companies all over the world. Together they made more than 170 contacts, traveled approximately 2 million miles, and put in 50,000 hours of study. The result was that this team didn't just reinvent the wheel, they reinvented everything! At Saturn, there would be no time clocks. Everyone would work together in teams. Saturn team members would have a voice in decisions, and a stake in Saturn's success. Manufacturing would utilize processes that had never been set into production, like lost-foam castings for engine blocks, heads, and cranks. They would build automatic and manual transmissions on the very same equipment lines, which had never been done before. And, they would revolutionize how a vehicle was marketed.

The study led to the creation of a unique partnership between management and the United Auto Workers and was eventually turned into a Memorandum of Agreement. The revolutionary, 28-page labor agreement—one that fits in a shirt pocket instead of the usual three-inch-thick binder—guaranteed UAW representation in every aspect of the business, from corporate communications to finance to sales, service, and marketing.

In January 1985, Saturn Corporation was born—the first new American car company in 40 years. Two months later, Saturn held its first customer workshop to find out what import owners really wanted in a small car.

Saturn revealed its first concept car to the GM board in

January 1986. The car was built in 100 workdays, a record for General Motors. Also in 1986, Richard G. "Skip" LeFauve was named Saturn's new president.

Spring Hill, Tennessee, was selected as the location of Saturn's new 4.3-million square-foot factory, and excavation began on a 200-acre portion of the 2,450-acre site in June 1986. Site preparation began with the removal of some 200 trees, which were transported to a nursery (to be later replanted around the office complex). Although 2.8 million cubic yards of dirt and 3.3 million cubic yards of rock were removed during this phase of construction, Saturn was committed to preserving the environment and minimizing construction impacts. In 1987, to protect the environment in Spring Hill, Saturn created its own Citizen Environmental Council.

By February 1989, the first 26 Saturn car dealers (soon to be known as "retailers") had been handpicked. Hal Riney & Partners, Saturn's advertising agency, took that opportunity to produce the first Saturn print advertisement, with a photo of the retail partners. The ad appeared in *Automotive News.*

The Launch

Finally, the day came. On July 30, 1990, the first Saturn rolled off the line at the plant in Spring Hill, Tennessee. GM chairman Roger B. Smith and UAW president Owen Bieber drove a medium-red metallic four-door sedan off the line at 10:57 A.M. It was officially launched from "Inspiration Point—shipping point for the world's best cars." On October 11, the first truckload of Saturns left the plant, bound for California.

The Saturn Difference

The entire Saturn "difference" is what I like best about Saturn. In particular, I like the way they design, build, and sell their cars; empower their workers; and care for their customers.

Charles Eickmeyer,
a Saturn admirer from the age of 10

The difference at Saturn is a company that emphasizes a "no-hassle, no-haggle" car buying experience. And a company that empowers employees—employees who enjoy their jobs and who strive to create enthusiastic customers. The difference is a unique partnership between all the people in the workforce, from assembly-line team members to engineers and retailers. The difference is an organizational structure that is represented by circles instead of the the conventional hierarchy. The difference is the Saturn/UAW Memorandum of Agreement, which states the following:

Structure and decision-making process reflects certain basic principles:

1. Recognition of stakes and equities of everyone in the organization being represented

2. Full participation by the representatives of the union

3. Use of consensus decision-making process

4. Placement of authority and decision-making in appropriate part of organization, with emphasis on work unit

5. Free flow of information

6. Clear definition of decision-making process

The difference is in selecting Saturn's retail facilities and working with those partners. (Notice that I didn't call them "dealerships." In an effort to change the whole image, Saturn determined that "retailers" or "retail facilities" presented a much more positive—and different—connotation.) Saturn uses a "market area approach," meaning that only one retailer occupies any given geographical area. The difference is in carefully designing Saturn's retail facilities. For example, where is a typical non-Saturn dealership's service department? Tucked away in the back, out of the customers' view. Not Saturn retail facilities. The sparkling clean and attractive service department is right up there next to the showroom. The waiting room for service customers is located right in the showroom. Now, that's different!

The difference is the ingenuity and high standards that go into designing and building the cars. The difference is an entire "Saturn experience" that results in enthusiastic, loyal customers. Customers who create their own Saturn car clubs. Customers who wear "I love my Saturn" T-shirts. Customers who create their own Saturn web sites on the Internet.

> *We've got two Saturns—only bought six months apart . . . and, well, our license plates are DIFF CO and DIFFCAR.*
> E. Chiasson, via e-mail

These Saturn differences are not by accident; they are by choice and hard work. The differences have accumulated over the years, and results have proven fruitful. A sampling of the many Saturn accolades, awards, and milestones is presented in Exhibit 2.1.

The Success

The Saturn success story continues. In terms of numbers, Saturn employs more than 9,700 people; has produced over 1.8 million cars; has 388 retail facilities in the United States plus sales in Taiwan, Canada, and Japan. Saturn plans to have over 500 retailers by the year 2000. And the car choices are growing too, with the introduction of a midsize model in 1999 and a sport-utility vehicle planned for 2002.

Saturn plans to continue its success story far into the future. Joe Kennedy, Saturn vice president for sales, service, and mar-

1990

July

- The first Saturn rolls off the line in Spring Hill, Tennessee, at 10:57 A.M. on July 30

November

- Saturn receives the Society of Plastics Engineers "1991 Automotive Division Grand Award" for the first thermoplastic exterior door panel.

- Breaking a record previously set by Mercedes-Benz in 1954, a car with a stock Saturn engine wins a four-hour endurance race at Sears Point Raceway.

December

- *Popular Science* magazine names Saturn one of "The Year's 100 Greatest Achievements in Science and Technology."

1991

January

- *Popular Mechanics* magazine confers its 1991 "Design and Engineering Award" on Saturn for manufacturing processes that yield high quality in an all-new vehicle.

Spring

- Saturn retailers hold their first customer picnics and service clinics to forge new relationships between owners and automobile facilities.

April

- Saturn receives two Silver Anvil Awards from the Public Relations Society of America for outstanding achievements in community relations and internal communications.

May

- *Home Mechanix* magazine gives Saturn its 1991 "Easy Maintenance Car of the Year" award.

Exhibit 2.1   Saturn Accolades, Awards, and Milestones

October

- Saturn cars go on sale in Canada.

December

- American Automobile Association (AAA) names the Saturn SC the best car in the $10,000 to $15,000 range.

1992

March

- Saturn ranks number one in sales per outlet, marking the first time in 15 years that a domestic brand holds the honor.

April

- PBS' *Motorweek* extends its "Driver's Choice Award" for best small car to Saturn—for the second year in a row.

June

- Saturn cars go on sale in Taiwan.

August

- Saturn forms a team of consultants—Saturn Consulting Services—to share the company's knowledge and experience with other branches of General Motors and with organizations around the world.

September

- *Kiplinger's Personal Finance* magazine adds another award to Saturn's shelf: "Best in Class under $10,000."
- Saturn is the highest-ranking domestic nameplate in the 1992 J.D. Power and Associates Customer Satisfaction Index.
- U.S. Department of Labor Secretary Lynn Martin gives Saturn the EVE (Exemplary Voluntary Efforts) Award for its work in recruiting women and minorities.

Exhibit 2.1   (continued)

December

- *Motor Trend* magazine names the Saturn SL one of the 1993 "Top Ten Domestic Buys."

1993

January

- Saturn receives the 1993 "Technology of the Year" award from *Automobile* magazine for developing an innovative traction control system at an affordable cost.

- *Consumers Digest* places the Saturn sedans and wagons on its list of "Best Buys in Compact Class."

- The Washington Automotive Press Association presents its 1993 "Golden Gear Award" to Saturn, "in recognition of outstanding contributions to the automotive industry."

March

- Saturn again posts the highest sales per outlet: 1,072 vehicles per retailer in 1992. (Honda was second with 654.)

- *Design News* magazine's "1993 Engineering Quality Award" is given to the Saturn line of vehicles in recognition of excellence in design, engineering, and manufacturing.

September

- Saturn builds its 500,000th car.

1994

January

- Saturn announces an operating profit for the calendar year 1993.

- IntelliChoice adds to the long list of awards with "Best American Car Value Under $13,000" and "Best Overall Value in the Compact Class under $16,500."

June

- Saturn hosts the "Homecoming" to celebrate the company's first five years—the first time ever that an auto manufacturer

Exhibit 2.1   (continued)

has invited all of its customers (over 600,000 at the time) for a visit to the factory. More than 44,000 take Saturn up on the offer, while another 130,000 participate in events at their local retailers throughout the summer.

- Saturn goes on-line with an interactive marketing program on the Prodigy computer service.

October

- GM's North American Operation announces the formation of the Small Car Group, formalizing a strategic relationship between Saturn and the Lansing Automotive Division, to share the best parts and technology from both programs. Saturn's president, Skip LeFauve, is named executive in charge of the new group.

1995

January

- Saturn announces record sales in 11 of 12 months during 1994. Total calendar-year sales of 286,000 vehicles represents a 25 percent increase over the 1993 calendar year.

June

- Saturn builds its 1-millionth car—a dark-green SC2.

August

- Saturn introduces its first major redesign, as the second-generation sedans and wagons debut.

- Donald W. Hudler is named president of Saturn Corporation. Hudler had been Saturn's vice president of sales, service, and marketing.

1996

January

- General Motors announces that it will produce the EV1 electric vehicle, to be distributed and marketed by Saturn.

Exhibit 2.1   (continued)

August

- Saturn completes the transition to second-generation models by introducing all-new coupes.

- GM, Saturn, and the UAW announce that Saturn will build a new-generation vehicle—a larger vehicle in the Saturn line—at a Wilmington, Delaware, facility.

December

- The first GM EV1 electric vehicles are delivered to customers through Saturn's 24 retailers serving Southern California and Arizona.

For the calendar year

- Saturn retailers sell more cars per facility than any other brand (for the fifth consecutive year) and rank sixth in retail sales among all automakers.

- J.D. Power and Associates:

- Sales Satisfaction Index—Saturn places number one overall, tied with Lexus.

- New Car Initial Quality Study—Saturn is sixth overall in terms of initial product quality, making it the top-rated domestic nameplate.

- Customer Satisfaction Index—Saturn is rated the number one domestic car. Overall, Saturn rates fourth, tied with Mercedes Benz, behind Infiniti, Lexus, and Acura.

1997

January

- A blue SC2 becomes the 1.5-millionth Saturn vehicle produced at Spring Hill.

April

- Saturn president Donald W. Hudler assumes the additional duty of chairman of Saturn Corporation. Skip LeFauve, Saturn's first chairman, becomes GM's senior vice president for

Exhibit 2.1 (continued)

global leadership development and global human resource processes.

- Saturn begins sales in Japan through 11 retailers.

May

- Saturn's new Welcome Center opens in Spring Hill—in a renovated horse barn that was once the home of a two-time grand champion Tennessee walking horse.

October

- Saturn announces adjustment of the manufacturer's suggested retail prices (MSRPs) on 1998 SL1 and SL1 sedans, and makes them retroactive to the start of sale of the 1998 model year.

For the year

- Despite declines in the market for small cars, Saturn is the fourth-best-selling car in retail sales.

  J.D. Power and Associates:

- Survey of Driver Satisfaction—Saturn is one of only two U.S. cars ranked in the top 10.

- Sales Satisfaction Index—for the third consecutive year, Saturn is named the "Best Overall Nameplate in Sales Satisfaction."

- Customer Satisfaction—Saturn is in seventh place (the top six are all luxury cars).

- Initial Quality Survey—shows the Saturn SL as the best in the "Premium Compact" segment. As a nameplate, Saturn is the top-rated domestic brand in initial quality, ranking in seventh place overall.

  IntelliChoice:

- Ranks the 1997 SL1, SL2, SC1, and SC2 models as the "Best Overall Values" in their respective classes. This marks the fifth consecutive year that Saturn has received the award for small, affordable vehicles. In fact, Saturn is the only manu-

Exhibit 2.1   (continued)

facturer to have every one of its cars recognized as "Best Values" in their class.

Kiplinger's *1997 Buyer's Guide*:

- "The New Cars" section rates the Saturn SL2 tops in three categories—"Best in Class," "Best in Resale Value," and "Best Cars under $13,000." The entire Saturn family of vehicles is rated "First in Safety."

1998

March

- Saturn workers vote to keep their unique labor agreement, by a margin of nearly 2 to 1.

Summer

- Saturn is the only GM plant in the United States producing cars, as union strikes shut down GM's North America plants. Saturn workers vote to give their union representatives authorization to strike against General Motors if necessary, but issues are resolved and a strike is averted.

September

- Saturn announces (subject to GM approval) the possible addition of a new sport utility vehicle, which could almost double annual capacity at its Spring Hill plant.

J.D. Power and Associates:

- Sales Satisfaction Survey—for the fourth consecutive year, Saturn ranks the highest. The rest of the top 10 are luxury nameplates, most of them foreign.

IntelliChoice:

- Selects six out of seven Saturns to the list of "Best Overall Values of the Year." For the sixth year in a row, a Saturn sedan wins an IntelliChoice "Best Overall Value" award, and for the fifth consecutive year the SL Series wins the "Best Overall Value" in its class.

Exhibit 2.1   (continued)

keting, reveals that "Our vision extends beyond the current market conditions. Quality, value, and service are cornerstones in the growth of a hundred-year car company."

A "DIFFERENT" THOUGHT

Over the past decade, the formation and operation of Saturn have been studied by many other companies and some government agencies who were looking for the secret to success. I believe one of the keys is that Saturn has dared to be different. That is, different from the ways that automotive manufacturers, their retailers, and the union have operated for decades. Different from the way most businesses treat their customers. But perhaps not so different from the way we were taught to treat other people, and the way we treat our friends. Maybe we just tend to forget to apply that consideration to customers in the business world.

By having the conviction to break out of an existing mold, with their "clean-sheet-of-paper" approach, good things have happened for Saturn. Do you have the conviction to do what it takes?

3

Creating Customer Loyalty: Where to Begin

You have to look at the whole picture: the car, sales, and service. What makes it special is that I feel I'm being treated like a human being. And that they care.

Al Clapsaddle,
with a total of 13 Saturns in the family
over the years

Just like loyal Saturn customer Al Clapsaddle says, you have to look at the whole picture. When it comes to creating customer loyalty, the "whole picture" means *the whole way* a company does business. To illustrate, let's look at Al's whole story from the beginning:

I had given up on buying American cars in 1990. Four years ago, when my son turned 16, he asked for my help in looking at cars. I didn't even know what a Saturn was. When I heard that it was an American car and you had to pay full sticker price, I said "No way!" My son pointed out that it wasn't right to be prejudiced about something that I didn't know anything about. So, I called the local Saturn retailer and ended up talking to the sales consultant for about *one hour*. She politely and patiently answered my questions. Now, I'm already thinking that this is different! I told her that I'd think about it and call back in about a week.

One week went by, and there was no call from the sales consultant that I thought for sure would be hounding me immediately. Strange, because salespeople usually don't want you to get away. Five minutes before closing, I called her, fully expecting that she wouldn't have time for me. Surprise again! She stayed on the phone for a half an hour after closing, answering my questions. There was absolutely no pressure. Now, I'm thinking, "There's something wrong with this!"

We finally went in to meet with her. I told her what we looking for and tried to start haggling. She showed me a price list and pleasantly described their no-haggle, no-hassle way of doing business. When it came time for a test drive, she went over everything about the car first. We ended up taking three or four cars out for a test drive. Each time, she patiently explained different features about each car. I wondered, "Where's the camera? There has to be some kind of gimmick."

My son wanted the Saturn, but it turned out that he couldn't afford it at that time. Know what happened? I ended up buying a Saturn for myself!

Today, we have seven Saturns in the family, counting two of my brothers and a sister in another state. Five of us are on our second Saturn. My wife of 25 years feels comfortable taking the car in for service by herself. My younger single sister doesn't have to get her brother to take the car in for service.

As you might guess—and as you are about to read—many factors are involved in creating customer loyalty. Yes, it is a challenge, but an exciting and rewarding one! Remember the list of "Ten Reasons To Create Customer Loyalty" in Chapter 1? Well, there's more to the story. So, before we tackle the how-to process, let me further convince you of the benefits.

Why Customer Loyalty Should Be Important to You

When I told fellow business friends that I was writing about creating customer loyalty, the responses were generally divided into two categories. In the first category were the ones who would roll their eyes and respond with something like, "Good luck—loyalty is dead, or next to impossible." True, customer loyalty is not what is was 50 years ago (so I'm told; I wasn't actually around to experience it myself). The second category, which I'm happy to say represented the majority, responded with more positive statements. "Great! I know we need to work at that, but we're just not sure how." Or, even better, "Loyal customers are a big part of why we've been successful in business all these years."

In today's competitive times, the search is really on for ways to create customer loyalty. Or if it's not, it should be. This is not the latest "management fad." It's a way of doing business—one that has been around for centuries. The sad truth is that many major corporations now lose *half* their customers in five years. And ignoring these losses can mean a bleak and shortened future for companies, not to mention reduced profits.

It's like a leaky bucket. As a company loses customers out of the leak in the bottom of the bucket, they have to continue to add new customers (an expensive process) to the top of the bucket. If the company can even partially plug the leak, the bucket stays fuller. It then takes fewer new customers added to the top of the bucket to achieve the same level of profitability. It's less expensive and more profitable to keep those customers already in the bucket.

Smart business people realize that it costs 5 to 10 times more to land a new customer than to keep a customer they already have. They also recognize that increasing the number of cus-

tomers they keep by a small percentage can *double* profits. And
it doesn't matter what type of business you have—the potential
for profits can be substantial. A study by Bain & Company,
Inc., cited in Frederick F. Reichheld's *The Loyalty Effect*,[2] looked
at a wide range of industries including insurance, advertising, banking, industrial distribution, office building management, and software. The study found that the impact of a
5-percentage-point increase in retention rate represented anywhere from a 35 percent to 95 percent increase in customer net
present value. For instance, if a credit card company can hold
on to another 5 percent of its customers each year (increasing
its retention rate from 90 percent to 95 percent), then the total
lifetime profits from a typical customer will rise, on average, by
75 percent. Reichheld expands on the "leaky bucket" comparison with the following example of long-term growth:

> Imagine two companies, one with a customer retention rate of 95
> percent, the other with a rate of 90 percent. The leak in the first
> firm's customer bucket is 5 percent per year, and the second firm's
> leak is twice as large, 10 percent per year. If both companies
> acquire new customers at the rate of 10 percent per year, the first
> will have a 5 percent net growth in customer inventory per year,
> while the other will have none. Over fourteen years, the first firm
> will double in size, but the second will have no real growth at all.

Reichheld's book goes further in charting the relationship
between customer retention and *productivity*, in addition to
profitability. The numbers and results are from real companies.
And the numbers are very impressive!

Then there's the "lifetime value" factor to consider. Carl Sewell
is one of the nation's leading Cadillac dealers (and of other
makes/models as well). In his book *Customers for Life*,[3] Sewell cal-
culates the amount of revenue an auto dealer could realize from
an average buyer if the dealership could keep the customer for
life. Would you believe . . . $332,000? That's just ONE customer!

In late 1997, at the same time that it was announced that Toyota's Camry was the number one selling car in the United States, other news articles were explaining Toyota's new tactics aimed at boosting customer loyalty. Even though sales were up and market share was increasing, Toyota in 1997 was rated below the industry average in the way it treats customers. Thus it seems that Toyota was worried that growth could falter if they couldn't keep more customers in the fold.

You don't have to be a huge corporation to be concerned about and benefit from customer loyalty. Even independent agents, consultants, and one-person companies will find that business is more rewarding (in more ways than one) when the focus is on creating customer loyalty. And for those of you who shudder over the thought of making sales calls, taking the loyalty road can ease your burden and turn those shudders into smiles.

The Mechanics of Customer Loyalty

I truly say Saturn people are the nicest I have ever dealt with—
anywhere.

Mary Chism,
a 76-year-young repeat Saturn buyer

I think a Saturn team member summed it pretty well when she said, "This is not rocket science. We're doing a lot of basic, simple things, but what customer loyalty all boils down to is the way that you treat people." Customers loudly echo that sentiment. The common theme running through my interviews with Saturn customers was that they like the way they're treated. "Like a friend" and "Like family" were oft-repeated phrases. Tom Peters, in his book *The Pursuit of WOW!*,[4] expressed his opinion that Saturn has created their almost cult-like following "by embracing the customer as a friend—an intelligent friend—from the moment the customer first steps into the showroom."

So, what's the "model" for customer loyalty? Here's my version. Picture a circle, or since we're talking Saturn, make that a wheel. The wheel starts with a simple statement at the top: Treat people right. The wheel then turns to produce loyal customers, which in turn provides increased profitability (see Exhibit 3.1).

It's not a flashy, detailed, polished chrome model, but it *can* be more valuable than gold! I believe that what it boils down to is this: Companies that live by the Golden Rule of treating people right—rather than focusing on profit—tend to make more money, grow faster, and survive longer.

There is no single solution for creating customer loyalty, just as there is no single car that pleases everyone. It's a combination of lots of little things that add up. Your business is different, customers are different, and there is a world of options from which to choose. But it is important for the "combination of lots of little things to fit together. A Jaguar engine in a Saturn SL1 just won't work. Here's how one manager at a Saturn retail facility sums up the process:

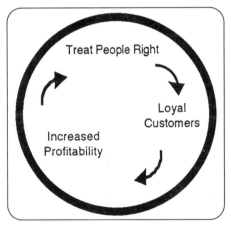

Exhibit 3.1   Model for Customer Loyalty

You make the guests comfortable, you welcome them into the facility, you interview them, find out what their wants and needs are, find out how we can satisfy them, show them that we have a vehicle that can meet or exceed their requirements, demonstrate the vehicle, consult on the purchase, handle the paperwork, get the car ready, they get to drive off the showroom floor . . . and that's when everything begins. And that's what's so different about Saturn. We're an experience that happens to come with the car.

You see, Saturn isn't just about building cars. It's about building a unique and powerful *relationship* between the people who build, sell, service, and own the cars. One of Saturn's brochures states that "it's not always easy to define what Saturn is or isn't. But we know it's more than a car. Or a car company. And it's probably more about all of us doing things together than anything else." In fact, the "treat people right" part of the customer loyalty model encompasses not only customers, but also team members (employees), retailers, suppliers, neighbors, and other stakeholders.

Whether you're a one-person business or the CEO of a multibillion-dollar conglomerate, it's up to you to create the excitement and the environment that are the building blocks for customer loyalty. It doesn't have to be complicated. In fact, you'll find that many of the customer loyalty ingredients are basic, common courtesies and common sense. But the concepts and practices have to be the core of a business, embraced by everyone in the company. So, where do you start? At the top, beginning with individual attitudes, management philosophy, and example-setting showing that customers do indeed come first. Of course, you have to consider whether the pursuit of loyalty is consistent with your own goals. Is it in your head, *and* in your heart?

You can't just pick and choose one or two things to try temporarily and hope it works. It won't. For example, in Chapter 8

you'll read abc _freebies_ ıl New Owner Clinics. A
Cadillac deale he clinics for their customers, and fai 's the Honda dealer that
tried the no-ha ONE weekend only.
Be forewarne ıstomer loyalty:

1. It must be earned.
2. It's not easy to gain or keep.
3. It doesn't happen overnight.
4. Keeping loyal customers and creating new ones is a continuous process.

If you're in business just to make a quick buck, this style is
not for you. But, if you believe in treating people right, developing long-term customers, and growing your business and profits in the process, then read on!

Creating Loyalty Starts With . . .

. . . the Mission and Philosophy. This is where everything starts
with Saturn. In Chapter 2, you read about the beginning mission and philosophy given the Group of 99. Once Saturn was
born, the mission and philosophy were further developed. Take
a look at Saturn's mission statement first (see Exhibit 3.2), and
notice that it doesn't stop short with just a belief. It spells out
"how to meet needs" in order to fulfill the mission.

Now take a look at Saturn's philosophy statement, and note
how it specifically addresses the needs of customers, team
members, suppliers, retailers, neighbors, and communities (see
Exhibit 3.3).

In the previous section, I warned that keeping loyal customers and creating new ones is a continuous process. Saturn
recognizes this, as is obvious by the closing statement of the
philosophy. Use of the word "operating" also implies that just

---

SATURN
MISSION

Earn the loyalty of Saturn
owners and grow our
family by developing and
marketing U.S.
manufactured vehicles that
are world leaders in quality,
cost and customer
enthusiasm through the
integration of people,
technology and business
systems.

Exhibit 3.2 Saturn Mission Statement

writing down a philosophy on a piece of paper doesn't do much good if it's never put into action.

And so the philosophy and process continue to develop. Saturn's "Customer Philosophy," which pretty much says it all about how to treat customers, is shown in Exhibit 3.4.

CUSTOMER ENTHUSIASM. It's definitely there. I've seen it and experienced it among Saturn customers. And I believe it evolves into loyal customers for Saturn.

SATURN PHILOSOPHY

We, the Saturn Team, in concert with the UAW and General Motors, believe that meeting the needs of Customers, Saturn Members, Suppliers, Retailers, Neighbors, and Investors is fundamental to fulfilling our mission.

To meet our customers' needs:
• Our products and services must be world leaders in value and satisfaction.

To meet our Members' needs:
• We will create a sense of belonging in an environment of mutual trust, respect and dignity.
• We believe that all people want to be involved in decisions that affect them, care about their jobs and each other, take pride in themselves and in their contributions and want to share in the success of their efforts.
• We will develop the tools, training and education for each member, recognizing individual skill and knowledge.
•We believe that creative, motivated, responsible team members who understand that change is critical to success are Saturn's most important asset.

To meet our Suppliers' and Retailers' needs:
• We will strive to create real partnerships with them.
• We will be open and fair in our dealings, reflecting trust, respect and their importance to Saturn.
• We want retailers and suppliers to feel ownership in Saturn's mission and philosophy as their own.

To meet the needs of our Neighbors, the communities in which we live and operate:
• We will be good citizens, protect the environment and conserve natural resources.
• We will seek to cooperate with government at all levels and strive to be sensitive, open and candid in all our public statements.

To meet the needs of all Saturn Investors:
• We will operate in a manner that promotes renewal and growth of the company and provides a competitive return for their investment and involvement in the business.

By continuously operating according to this philosophy, we will fulfill our mission.

Exhibit 3.3   Saturn Philosophy Statement

Sharing the Message

Saturn has its mission, philosophies, and values printed on three-by-five-inch cards, which are widely distributed to team members and elsewhere. They appear on posters. They're framed and hang in hallways, conference rooms, and retail facil-

**CUSTOMER
PHILOSOPHY**

We, the Saturn Team, believe the single most important element of our business is the Customer ...therefore, we must be Customer focused in everything we do.

To be truly successful, our sights must be aimed beyond providing Customer satisfaction, we must exceed Customer expectations and provide an unparalleled buying and vehicle ownership experience that results in CUSTOMER ENTHUSIASM.

If a Saturn Customer requires information or assistance, we believe it provides us an opportunity to demonstrate that SATURN CARES about them.

Above all else, treat Customers the way they wish to be treated.

By continuously operating in accordance with our philosophy, we will stimulate positive word-of-mouth advertising, achieve conquest sales, create strong owner loyalty, and most importantly, achieve CUSTOMER ENTHUSIASM.

Exhibit 3.4   Saturn Customer Philosophy Statement

ity showrooms. They're posted on Saturn's web site. Plus, they are taught in a three-day course at Spring Hill, which you'll read about in the next chapter. In other words, they are shared and they are visible. What good does it do if these things are only in the mind of the president, or mentioned once a year at the annual meeting?

WHAT YOU CAN DO

Where to Begin

Saturn had the luxury of beginning this process from scratch, using a clean-paper approach. On the other hand, you're probably already in business. But you don't have to start over. Instead, start fresh—with a snapshot evaluation of just where you are on the road to creating customer loyalty. Exhibit 3.5 is my checklist to get you started. Check off the items where you believe you're already there. The blanks will tell you where you need to focus. But keep in mind that, even if you are the boss, it's not just your opinion that counts. Bravely seek out evaluations from your employees, and even suppliers. You will notice that employees are just as much a part of the list as are customers.

The status checklist is designed to get you thinking—and to keep you reading to discover how to make it all happen. And whether you have just a few blank boxes or quite a few, there's always room for improvement!

❑ Company mission and philosophy are in writing (give yourself a bonus point if they include statements regarding customers and employees).

❑ Company mission and philosophy are shared with all employees.

❑ Philosophies are translated into five or six core values to do business by.

❑ Values are embraced and practiced by employees.

❑ Management sets the examples necessary for a customer-focused company culture.

Exhibit 3.5   Status Checklist for Creating Customer Loyalty

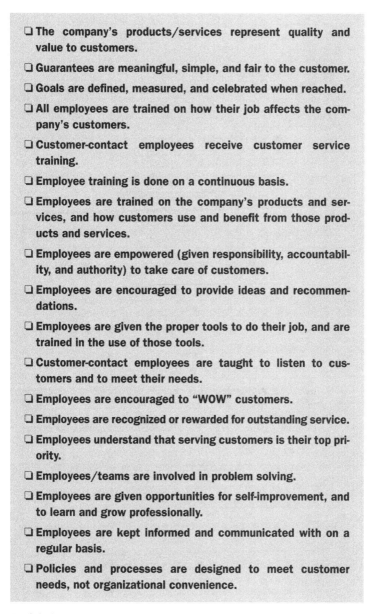

❏ The company's products/services represent quality and value to customers.

❏ Guarantees are meaningful, simple, and fair to the customer.

❏ Goals are defined, measured, and celebrated when reached.

❏ All employees are trained on how their job affects the company's customers.

❏ Customer-contact employees receive customer service training.

❏ Employee training is done on a continuous basis.

❏ Employees are trained on the company's products and services, and how customers use and benefit from those products and services.

❏ Employees are empowered (given responsibility, accountability, and authority) to take care of customers.

❏ Employees are encouraged to provide ideas and recommendations.

❏ Employees are given the proper tools to do their job, and are trained in the use of those tools.

❏ Customer-contact employees are taught to listen to customers and to meet their needs.

❏ Employees are encouraged to "WOW" customers.

❏ Employees are recognized or rewarded for outstanding service.

❏ Employees understand that serving customers is their top priority.

❏ Employees/teams are involved in problem solving.

❏ Employees are given opportunities for self-improvement, and to learn and grow professionally.

❏ Employees are kept informed and communicated with on a regular basis.

❏ Policies and processes are designed to meet customer needs, not organizational convenience.

Exhibit 3.5 (continued)

❏ Employees and customers take pride the the company image.

❏ The company recognizes the value of teamwork, and teams are formed and utilized accordingly.

❏ The company strives beyond customer satisfaction.

❏ The company celebrates customers and their purchases.

❏ Technologies for delivering the best customer service possible are evaluated and utilized as appropriate.

❏ New prospects are not offered special deals that would make existing customers feel neglected or cheated.

❏ The company has some type of customer recognition, appreciation, reward, frequent buyer, or preferred customer program in place.

❏ The company recognizes long-term customer value.

❏ The company values customer information by managing it, protecting it, and using it to help customers.

❏ The company evaluates customer contact points and makes improvements accordingly.

❏ Customers are encouraged to provide input.

❏ It's easy for customers to do business with the company— every step of the way.

❏ Customers are consulted on prospective changes and regarding their wants and needs.

❏ The company tracks and acknowledges or rewards customer referrals.

❏ Technology use is customer-friendly.

❏ Existing customers are communicated with on a regular basis.

❏ Customer complaints and problems are used as learning opportunities.

Exhibit 3.5 (continued)

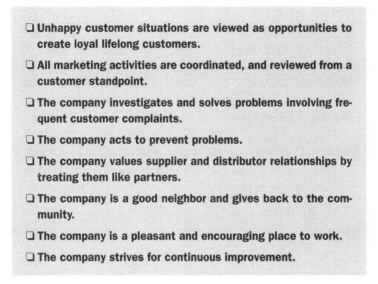

❑ Unhappy customer situations are viewed as opportunities to create loyal lifelong customers.

❑ All marketing activities are coordinated, and reviewed from a customer standpoint.

❑ The company investigates and solves problems involving frequent customer complaints.

❑ The company acts to prevent problems.

❑ The company values supplier and distributor relationships by treating them like partners.

❑ The company is a good neighbor and gives back to the community.

❑ The company is a pleasant and encouraging place to work.

❑ The company strives for continuous improvement.

Exhibit 3.5   (continued)

What comes next? How are all these words put into action? It's through adherence to five basic values, which you are about to read in the next chapter. Values that are not only taught to all Saturn team members and sought in new-hires, but values that are lived each day by every team member. Throughout Part Two, you will witness how these values are further defined, represented, and reinforced, resulting in customer loyalty.

STEP UP AND LOOK IN

Be ready to open your mind to a different way of doing business and treating customers. For some, the step up to customer loyalty is equivalent to a flying leap over the Grand Canyon. For others, it's just the next short rung on a six-foot ladder. As you proceed, I encourage you to look at your business with what I call my "LenzSight." Think of an eyeglass lens, and imagine looking at your business through the lens—from the customers' point of view. Then, translate the insights you gain into changes and improvements in your business, all the while maintaining customer focus.

CHAPTER
4

Building on Core Values

The spirit of the relationship was and continues to be that we look at our partnership as a marriage, and much like any marriage, things don't always work out. But you certainly go into it with the approach that it's a lifelong commitment. There will be bumps in the road, and if you work on communicating, and you work according to the vision and commitment that you made at the outset, then those partnerships can blossom and grow and bear tremendous fruit in the future.

Company President, a Saturn Supplier

That quote pretty well sums up not only the ideal supplier relationship, but also applies to customers and employees. Since the key here is treating people right, we must consider all the "people" involved in the customer-loyalty process. And we must realize that, like a marriage, the process is not perfect. Nor is any process perfect. But it starts with commitment. And it takes some assembly to put all the pieces together and make the process work.

Some clarification might be in order here. Please, don't try to BE Saturn. That's not what this book is all about. As much as Saturn is "a different kind of company," so is your company. Your products and services are different; your employees and customers are different. There's an old saying about how it's better to teach people how to fish than just to give them a fish dinner. Consider this a fishing lesson.

Creating customer loyalty is not an easy or quick process. It takes time and perseverance, not short-term thinking. A Saturn team member offered a good analogy about a farmer that plants his field full of seeds. It may seem like the field just sits dormant for months, with nothing happening. But if the farmer digs it up too soon, in order to try something different, he has ruined everything.

Saturn prepared their field with the mission statement and philosophies you saw in Chapter 3. Then they added one more element to ensure that the field begins and remains fertile: *core values.* This set of five values truly represents the Saturn way of doing business:

- Commitment to customer enthusiasm
- Commitment to excel
- Teamwork
- Trust and respect for the individual
- Continuous improvement

Loyalty is not just about customers, and policies are not what makes a company competitive. We're talking about principles— in the form of core values. Loyalty to a set of values is what enables a business to thrive over time.

We're now ready to examine these five values in a little more detail, one at a time. Each Saturn value and definition is presented; the "how it works" interpretations that follow are solely mine, based on my observations of how Saturn does business.

Commitment to Customer Enthusiasm

We continually exceed the expectations of internal and external customers for products and services that are world leaders in cost, quality, and customer satisfaction. Our customers know that we really care about them.

Notice that the first word in this value is *commitment* and the first word of the explanation is *we*. That is the beginning of what it takes to create customer loyalty. At the top, from the top, then involving everybody. Enough said.

Exceed the expectations rather than just meeting expectations is one difference between having loyal customers versus simply having satisfied customers. *Continually exceed* means it has to be practiced every day.

Internal customers is one of my favorites. These are our coworkers, team members, fellow employees, associates, or whatever term you use. In another book, I refer to internal customers as costars, because every single person plays a starring role in the big picture of serving both internal and paying (external) customers. I found one dictionary definition of "customer" as "an individual with whom one must deal." Sure sounds like a coworker to me. One Saturn team member told me about his early training at Spring Hill, where customers were identified as more than just end-customers. A customer was defined as "anyone who takes a product from you." Each participant in the training program developed their own "customer-supplier relationship" form, and went to the persons both upstream and downstream to complete the form. Upstream, the question was "I'm your supplier; what do you need from me?" Downstream, the statement was "I'm your customer; here's what I need from you." It's an exercise that makes an impression, especially on employees that aren't exposed to the end customer. When coworkers start applying the two Golden Rules of customer loyalty (in Chapter 6) amongst themselves, that is a huge step in the right direction towards creating end-customer loyalty.

Products and services apply because you provide both, no matter what your business. The word "product" refers not only to some "thing" but also means "a direct result." To provide products and services *that are world leaders in cost, quality* means that you have to provide VALUE to customers.

Our customers know that we really care about them. In our wheel model of customer loyalty (Chapter 3), we start off with and keep coming back to "treat people right." In other words, *care.* Sixty-eight percent of the customers who leave a company do so because they perceive that the company is indifferent to their needs. Customers *know* you care only if you continually communicate and demonstrate that spirit to them through thoughts, words, and actions. Later in this chapter, you will see how this particular value translates into six steps for customer enthusiasm.

SATURN CORE VALUE

Commitment to Excel

There is no place for mediocrity and half-hearted efforts at Saturn. We accept responsibility, accountability and authority for overcoming obstacles and reaching beyond the best. We choose to excel in every aspect of our business, including return on investment.

Excel takes on additional meaning at Saturn, in the form of an outdoor program called the Excel Course. It teaches people that they can do more than they think they can, and helps people believe in themselves.

When there is *no place for mediocrity and half-hearted efforts,* people know they must strive to do their best. Whatever the task at hand, you owe it to yourself to give 100-percent effort. Saturn strives to ensure employee commitment by hiring the right people in the first place. There is no personnel department to do the hiring. Instead, teams or representatives from teams are involved in the interview process, which includes a structured assessment process. For example, the Sales, Service & Marketing team in Spring Hill forms a three-member internal team to interview a candidate for the field organization. The team consists of a person from a Saturn retail facility, a regional team leader (from one of Saturn's four defined regions of the country), and a home office team leader. The prospective candidate is evaluated on things like problem-solving, leadership, and decision-making skills. Open-ended questions are used, such as, "Tell us about the time you disagreed with someone, and what you did to change their mind." Each team member ranks responses on a numbered scale. At the end of the process, all three members have to reach consensus on each score. Then the team presents their recommendation to management. The thoroughness of the process serves to improve morale and reduce turnover (a low 6 to 8 percent average for the marketing team). It's important to find people that are likely to fit into your company culture, because the ones that don't fit will have a hard time at excelling, and won't stay long.

We accept is to ask the question like "How can we find a way to do that?" instead of simply responding, "No, we can't do that."

Three words that go together: *responsibility, accountability and authority.* Don't give one without the other two. One way that Saturn puts these three words together is through their "Risk & Reward" program. Everyone is on salary—even union team members. Under this program, a certain percentage of their salary is "at risk," meaning that everyone must meet certain goals in order to earn their full salary. For example, if 12 percent of their salary is at risk, the breakdown and goals might look like this:

5 percent—*Quality of product*	This is typically measured based on a combination of audits performed both internally and independently. (Read more on quality in Chapter 5.)
5 percent—*Training*	Every team member is required to complete a minimum of 92 hours of training per year. Most of the training is available in-house. (Details on training are throughout Part Two.)
2 percent—*Team effectiveness*	This may be measured based on participation in quarterly team communication meetings and team-building sessions. (More on teams in this section under the "Teamwork" value.)

Team members can also be rewarded with an above-average salary, based on other elements like production, quality, and financial performance of the company. The goals are negotiated each year. They are targeted at meeting Saturn's overall goals, not to put groups or divisions in competition with each other. So, you see, everyone does indeed have responsibility, accountability, and authority, which contribute to the company excelling.

As you might imagine, compensation plans in a no-hassle environment at the retail level tend to be different. Saturn cars are usually sold at manufacturer's suggested retail price (MSRP), which includes a flat-fee commission per car. This helps drive sales consultants' behavior toward filling customer needs, rather than to driving up the car price to make a higher commission. Saturn retailers are independent business owners, so Saturn can't tell them how to pay salespeople. Instead, Saturn might suggest compensation packages and share best practices or ideas that work among retailers. Some retailers pay their sales consultants a higher fee per car after the team meets a set goal for car sales. Some pay a salary only. Others combine both methods to pay on some type of a risk/reward program, and they may utilize survey results as part of the equation. A part of Saturn's allocation system—used to determine the number of cars that go to each retail facility—is driven by how well customers are treated (surprise!). Retailers are continually evaluated against standard scores. Scores below an acceptable range signal problems. Likewise, there is incentive to earn more cars with high scores.

Responsibility, accountability, and authority also apply to employers in another way. A Saturn manager offered his insight in this area: "The team members' job is to bring the seeds of shared values, honesty, and integrity. Our job is to provide a fertile environment for those seeds to grow. People generally have the seeds, but most companies don't provide a fertile environmental for those seeds to grow." Just like I mentioned at the beginning of this chapter, company leaders have the responsibility, accountability, and authority to establish and live by principles.

Solving problems is what *overcoming obstacles* is all about. Don't just solve the problem; go the extra mile and you'll be *reaching beyond the best.*

You've heard it before: *success is a choice.* It is also the title of a book by Rick Pitino, a very successful basketball coach, and former coach of the University of Kentucky national championship team. Teams and individuals choose to succeed. *We choose to excel in every aspect* is your choice to make.

Another key spoke in the customer loyalty wheel is money, *including return on investment.* Increased profitability. Yes, you are in business to make a profit, otherwise you couldn't stay in business. Saturn has been profitable since 1993, but actually, the first money Saturn ever earned was not from cars. It was from soybeans. When it established its Spring Hill facility, Saturn pledged to continue farming the 1,300 acres of fertile land surrounding the factory. The first chapter of this book pointed out profit possibilities resulting from customer loyalty. So, farm your own fields of customers, and in return, loyalty will bring you return on investment.

SATURN CORE VALUE

Teamwork

We are dedicated to singleness of purpose through the effective involvement of members, suppliers, retailers, neighbors and other stakeholders. A fundamental tenet of our philosophy is the belief that effective teams engage the talents of individual members while encouraging team growth.

Teamwork is crucial in incorporating the other values. One common acronym for TEAM is: *Together Everyone Achieves More.* Saturn's whole manufacturing process is based on teams. Before a decision is made, all the teams talk about it first, and decisions are reached by consensus. They recognize that even a small change on the assembly line can affect all of the other people in all of the other teams. When hiring, they look for people who can work well in a team environment. Teams work, because regardless of the number of people on a team, they *are dedicated to singleness of purpose.* Saturn was born as a result of the work of one large team—The Group of 99. To accomplish the group's purpose, each member was assigned to one of seven teams. This group of teams definitely worked. It's impossible for me to imagine any one individual even coming close to achieving what this group did with teamwork.

Everyone is on a team at Saturn. Teams are self-directed and operate independently of or interdependently with other teams. A work unit at the plant is defined as an integrated group of approximately 6 to 15 team members. Each work unit has 30 functions. I want to share the basics of these functions with you because (1) I believe they illustrate how Saturn's mission, philosophy, and other values are intertwined, and because (2) together they add up to creating customer loyalty, whether the customer is internal (the next person or team on the line) or external (the car buyer).

The 30 Work Unit Functions

1. Reach decisions by consensus
2. Self-managed work units
3. Make their own job assignments
4. Resolve conflicts
5. Plan work
6. Design jobs
7. Control scrap
8. Control material and inventory
9. Perform incidental equipment maintenance
10. Schedule direct and indirect work
11. Schedule their communications within and outside the group
12. Keep their own records
13. Select new members of the unit

14. Constantly seek improvement in quality, cost, and work environment
15. Perform to their own budget
16. Integrate horizontally with business unit resources
17. Reflect synergistic group growth
18. Determine methods
19. Schedule relief
20. Schedule vacation
21. Provide absentee replacements
22. Perform their own repairs
23. Perform housekeeping
24. Maintain and perform their health and safety program
25. Be responsible for producing quality products to schedule at competitive costs
26. Assist in developing and delivering training
27. Obtain supplies
28. Seek resources as needed
29. Schedule and hold their own meetings
30. Initiate the consultation process for self-corrective action, with responsibility on the individual members

Effective teams at Saturn set standards for effectiveness, starting with having the team develop norms of behavior (i.e., reaching consensus as a group on how the team will in operate in meetings and on a day-to-day basis). Members are trained on how to work together as a team. They participate in team-building exercises, both in the classroom and on Spring Hill's Excel course. Classroom training might include a three-day course on building high-performance teams. Participants of this course learn how to:

- Leverage team members differences
- Create a supportive, success-charged environment
- Listen reflectively
- Manage time and tasks
- Plan, organize and think creatively through mind mapping
- Resolve conflict with team members
- Facilitate group decision making

The Excel Course is an outdoor program, and each team goes through the course. The program gives team members a chance to take risks and support one another. One part of the course has a 30-foot pole that each team member must climb, with the aid of another member (and by harnesses and safety ropes). The goal is to get to the top of the pole, turn 180 degrees on a rotating platform, jump off, and ring a bell. It brings teams together and produces a great sense of pride—results that carry over to their daily performance.

Encouraging team growth is also accomplished with awards for excellence. Team members each have a small budget to be used for these awards, given by and for individuals and teams. About 90 percent of the budget is earmarked for individual awards, for team members that go above and beyond the call of duty. The remainder goes towards a team award. For example, each team member may have a budget of $50. Out of that, $40 is for an individual award, and $10 can go towards a team award. One such team award was made—in cash—when an entire team decided to learn sign language, to help them communicate with a fellow team member who was deaf. Individual awards vary, but might be things like T-shirts or restaurant gift certificates.

Effectiveness and encouragement go beyond individual teams to encompass the whole *we.* At some car manufacturers, there are separate cafeterias for management and UAW members, but not at Saturn. All team members can sit down at the same tables for lunch every day.

Effective involvement means that you can't just pay lip service, and people are only grudgingly involved when it's forced on them. When workers, or members, have a true partnership with management, with a stake in the company's profitability and encouragement to be involved in shaping the company, it's only natural for them to take a more active role. They care more about the product they make or the services they provide. And happy, involved workers do make better cars, or widgets, or whatever.

Saturn effectively involves everyone: *members, suppliers, retailers, neighbors and other stakeholders.* When one company was originally sourced as a Saturn *supplier* in late 1980, it experienced a unique educational process long before being selected. At that time, the potential supplier was a young company, and Saturn was pretty progressive for the industry. The supplier first went through a two-phase process of responding to written questionnaires. This was not the typical "tell us exactly what you will charge and how you will do it" selection process. Both questionnaires asked a lot of questions about the supplier's philosophy and values—to determine, on the front end, if there would be a fit with the Saturn vision. Then, in the Saturn way, the selection process involved an interdisciplinary team of Saturn people, representing all of the different functional areas of the business. The Saturn team met with the supplier company officials to discuss the previously-submitted questionnaires. They also sought the supplier's definitions and feelings about partnerships and people development. Several members of the Saturn team also visited a couple of the supplier's customers. The supplier felt that Saturn "went to great lengths to make us understand the challenge that was ahead, and the excitement of the opportunity. So, in effect, they were trying to help us self-select whether we felt we were up to the task."

That same supplier has now witnessed *effective involvement* over the years. Its on-site team members sit in on any kind of committee that would be appropriate for them to be a part of at Saturn. For instance, they were intimately involved with planning and execution of the 1994 Homecoming. They're treated as an equal part of the Saturn team, not as an after-thought contractor.

Effective involvement means that supplier partners have a stake in the business. Great companies keep their edge with strong partnerships. When Saturn looks for parts suppliers for future vehicles, the Marketing and Product Planning team looks for companies that have not only the technology for today, but also have the depth in resources that will enable them to grow in technology and support. Saturn needs these suppliers to be a contributing part of the project development team. To help ensure effective involvement, Saturn enters into long-term, sometimes even lifetime contracts with selected suppliers. Some service suppliers are even on a Risk & Reward program with Saturn, similar to the employee program. Now that's a true vested interest. As one Saturn team member put it, "We like to say that our suppliers are partnerships with expectations. We've got to continue to earn the partnership and produce."

To start off on the right foot, Saturn selects its *retailers* (among other ways) by using a "market area approach." This approach means there is only one retailer for a given geographical area, not four or five dealerships in the same city competing against each other. Saturn recognizes that rather than competing with each other, retailers need to be profitable in order to deal with customers effectively and afford what it takes to develop relationships. Retailers are effectively involved on a variety of Saturn task forces and teams dealing with operations, planning, development, leadership, and so on. Plus, groups of retailers from different areas of the country get together on their own to talk and share ideas.

An important part of Saturn's business philosophy is "to meet the needs of our *neighbors* and communities in which we live and operate." Saturn and its retailers are good corporate citizens. It fits their value system. The list of Saturn's community involvement is almost endless, but here are some highlights:

- *Camp Fish Tales.* One retailer in Michigan joined with Saturn UAW members and local labor groups to raise nearly $500,000 to make the dream of this wonderful facility come true. It's a special barrier-free camp for children and adults with disabilities.

- *Cycle/recycle.* This is an ongoing community program, with participating retailers throughout the country serving as collection points for donated bicycles. The discarded bikes are restored and distributed to charitable organizations.

- *Excellence in education.* Saturn sponsors this multifaceted program designed to promote self-awareness and build self-esteem among American youth through partnerships with schools.

- *Inner-City Youth (ICY) Racing.* Race car driver Dave Rosenblum hand-picks teens from Edison High School, a tough Philadelphia neighborhood, to serve as members of his pit crew. He selects kids who get good grades and stay out of trouble. The teens not only gain knowledge of cars and enthusiasm for racing but also come away with values like teamwork and personal responsibility. More than 85 young people have gone through the program, but it doesn't stop there. Saturn retailers across the country have helped the ICY racing team by hosting events and arranging visits to local schools and youth groups. As a result, Dave has talked to more than 10,000 kids, spreading his "Winning in Life" message.

- *The Nature Conservancy.* In 1994, Saturn entered a partnership to assist this group with its continuing work to protect endangered natural areas throughout the United States and the world.

- *Saturn Playgrounds.* Saturn retailers donate money, time, and labor to construct children's playgrounds in areas of need. Since the project's beginning in 1993, close to 100 playgrounds have been constructed in communities that have included Atlanta, Chicago, Detroit, New York, and San Francisco, and as well as Canadian cities.

- *National Donor Day.* For Valentine's Day 1997, Saturn teamed up with its UAW partners and a group of health organizations to host National Donor Day. Retailers all over the country participated, and the day was a big success. They collected upwards of 6,000 units of blood, handed out some 3,000 organ and tissue donor cards, and added nearly 1,000 names to a national list of potential marrow donors. In all, about 12,000 people took the opportunity to learn more about the Five Points of Life of blood and organ donation.

All of this sort of involvement does indeed *engage the talents of individual members while encouraging team growth.*

SATURN CORE VALUE

Trust and Respect for the Individual

We have nothing of greater value than our people! We believe that demonstrating respect for the uniqueness of every individual builds a team of confident, creative members possessing a high degree of initiative, self-respect and self-discipline.

Trust is the foundation upon which relationships are built. I have *trust and respect* for all the individuals associated with Saturn, for they are what makes customer loyalty possible. Just as employees are in your organization. When the Group of 99 did their fact-finding visits before Saturn was formed, one common thread they observed among successful companies was this: *People will work together toward common goals under the right atmosphere of mutual trust and respect.*

You can't apply "treating people right" to groups of people without first applying it to individuals. And if you're not treating your individual employees right, don't expect them to treat customers right. *We have nothing of greater value than our people!* Not equipment, not technology, not products. You must have trust and respect for your people if you expect to earn the trust and respect of customers.

> *Saturn has adopted a different paradigm, a bone-deep belief in people, in people's potential, and therefore, they create opportunities for people to participate in the company.*
>
> Stephen R. Covey,[5]
> *author of The Seven Habits of Highly Effective People*

Even in a team-based environment, trust and respect start with individuals. Ideas, suggestions, and contributions are more likely to come from individuals that are *confident* and have *a high degree of initiative.* But many individuals need to be encouraged along these lines. The environment and leadership at Saturn combine to do just that. Teams help ensure that individuals are listened to and ideas are encouraged. "I Make the Difference" lapel pins are only one way that team members are recognized for their individual contributions.

Once a year, through "member-to-member communications," every team member at Saturn is talked with one-on-one, face-to-face, to find out concerns, likes, and dislikes. It's like an annual review, with the team member receiving feedback on performance by a team member reviewer. Saturn has recently started to try a different approach, giving the individual being reviewed the option of choosing their own review team. For example, an individual in Sales, Service and Marketing choosing this option would pick a team consisting of four to six people. But not just any people; the team must include a retail customer, a coworker, and someone from leadership. Everyone receives a copy of the appraisal form, which lists items covering four to five skill sets, for rating. And, in the Saturn team way, the team must reach a consensus on the ratings.

But that's just part of the continuous process of *demonstrating respect* for every individual. For instance, when a team reaches consensus on a decision (on any matter), every person in the room should be 70 percent comfortable with the decision. An individual who is not comfortable can challenge that decision IF he or she can come up with suggestions. Once agreement is reached, everyone on the team is expected to support the decision. This helps encourage individuals not only to think creatively, but also to practice *self-discipline.*

A couple of Saturn team members demonstrated their *creative* skills by figuring out a way to reduce waste. By sorting and sending back to the manufacturer for reuse the orange and black shipping caps that come off air-conditioner compressors, they saved the company more than $30,000 a year.

Another way of demonstrating respect for individuals can be found in the production process. Instead of struggling to attach parts to a car that's passing by on a conveyor belt, factory technicians can move with the car by riding on "skillets," which are comfortable wooden platforms. Skillets come with pneumatic lifts, which means the technicians can raise and lower the entire car to the height most ergonomically comfortable for them.

The way Saturn sees it, the happier team members are, the happier customers will be in the end. And Saturn team members don't see it as just doing a job. One team member explained it to me this way: "It's doing a job from the heart versus doing it because you have to have a job."

SATURN CORE VALUE

Continuous Improvement

We know that sustained success depends on our ability to continually improve the quality, cost and timeliness of our products and services. We are providing opportunity for personal, professional and organizational growth and innovation for all Saturn stakeholders.

Sustained success means that you can't rest on your past success. Continuous improvement is essential in keeping the wheel turning, and in keeping customers.

One of the ways that Saturn manages to *continually improve* is through continuous learning, evident by participation of every team member in 92 hours of training each year. For example, 24 hours of training might be devoted to team development. Right-to-Know is required training dealing with hazardous chemicals in the workplace. In-house courses are available on Stephen R. Covey's *The Seven Habits of Highly Effective People.* Plus, each individual plans a portion of his or her required training hours to improve their on-the-job skills. It might focus on sharpening computer, presentation, interpersonal, or leadership skills. Most of the training is available on-site, but some off-site conferences and workshops may be included.

The learning continues from lots of sources, including customers, retailers, suppliers, and competitors. Saturn is constantly benchmarking (i.e., measuring other companies' products or processes according to specified standards in order to compare with and improve its own, as you'll see in Chapter 5). So the next time you see a member of Saturn's planning team driving around town in a competitor's brand new car, chalk it up to benchmarking.

Goal setting and performance measurement is a big part of continuous improvement. Every team sets standards and measures performance, and tracks its own performance through charts and graphs and boards that seem to be posted everywhere. For instance, a large board in the Customer Assistance Center indicates monthly and year-to-date measurements against "key success factors" like training, correspondence, phone calls, and case quality. Each factor is assigned a goal in terms of a percentage or number that can be measured.

Sharing information throughout the company aids in the *improvement* process. Much of this work falls to the dozen or so members of Saturn's corporate communications team. They are responsible for media relations, product publicity, and community, industry, and government relations. However, 70 percent of their strategy is focused on internal communications. They strongly feel that creating an information-driven culture tends to reduce rumors and gossip by helping people understand the business objectives. One form of internal communication produced by the corporate communications team is the daily *Newsline,* a one-sheet, two-page paper that talks about the business. Many people depend on this form of communication, to the point that if it's a half-hour late in distribution, the phones start ringing in the corporate communications department. *Newsline* gives manufacturing and sales updates, covers safety issues, announces industry survey results, tells what groups are scheduled to tour the plant during the week, and everything else that team members would want or need to know. *Newsline* voice mail and internal computer mail are other forms of communication, along with a biweekly video production. "Windows On Saturn" is a 20- to 30-minute video produced at the full-scale studio on site at Spring Hill, with the help of EDS, a corporate partner. The video brings to life many of the same topics that are covered in *Newsline,* along with interviews with team members and leaders. Also shown are some community news and retailer events, like the building of a playground by Saturn folks. About 400 television monitors throughout the plant broadcast the video, plus all sorts of information almost around the clock. New in 1998 is a 15-minute video series, produced on alternate weeks, titled "To the Point." Each one is an interview with one of Saturn's leaders on a specific topic.

As Saturn people continue to improve their product and learn to better serve their customers, they believe in sharing this knowledge, thereby providing opportunities for *organizational growth* for other companies. Saturn University was formed to assist their retailers. Another Saturn group—Saturn Consulting Services—was formed in 1992 to share the knowledge with other organizations, both in General Motors and outside. This group of consultants, trainers, writers, and a lot of other talented people offer assistance (both on and off site) in the areas of leadership and team development, customer enthusiasm, and skills development. They also provide collaborative consulting, and the design, development, and delivery of customer services.

Just one more statement about *quality.* Saturn does not have a quality department. EVERYONE is responsible for quality.

There are always opportunities for *personal, professional, and organizational growth and innovation* at Saturn. Instead of a personnel or human resources department at Spring Hill, there is a People Systems team assisting others in these opportunities. Many positions offer the possibility of cross training, or moving cross-functionally. Career paths can be mapped out. There are opportunities to work on a task force. Tuition assistance programs are available for bachelor and master degree programs, and approximately 5 to 7 percent of the workforce take advantage of this annually. The percentage may seem low, but remember that degree programs are in addition to the expected 92-plus training hours per year. There are professional development opportunities in which some of the top people are chosen for three-month assignments at different GM plants—perhaps even overseas. This gives an individual a chance to experience and learn from how things are done elsewhere. These opportunities are all part of Saturn's belief that training is an investment—in the individual and in the growth of the company—not an expense. The investment pays off in *innovations,* such as the 82 patents that Saturn has under its belt.

· · ·

Those are the five Saturn values. They're pretty basic, but extremely important. My interpretations of how I see them working are merely a few specks of paint in the overall picture. More important is that the values are evident in the way Saturn does business, and when talking with individuals at Saturn. Values must be pursued not only by management, but by everyone in a company. And just as the mission and philosophies appear everywhere on posters and three-by-five-inch cards, so do the values. They're more than reminders. They become ingrained and a part of everyday work life.

Saturn offers initial training at Spring Hill on the company's culture and values, not only for on-site team members, but also for retail team members. The three-day course begins with orientation on how Saturn began and some historical milestones. Then participants explore the five core values in depth, and gain a valuable perspective on how to translate them into everyday work behaviors. Retail team members also spend time at the Excel Course, receive a plant tour, and interact with UAW partners, gaining experiences that are integral to the Saturn culture.

So, how do those values further translate to creating customer loyalty? Witness Saturn's "Six Steps to Customer Enthusiasm" (see Exhibit 4.1).

Throughout Part Two, we'll explore in greater detail how these steps work (before, during, and after the purchase) to create customer loyalty.

SIX STEPS TO CUSTOMER ENTHUSIASM

1. **LISTEN** to your Customers ... **don't assume; ask** ... seek to understand their specific needs, desires and expectations.

2. Create an environment of **MUTUAL TRUST** ... be **caring** and **responsive** to Customer requests. Be **honest** and timely, do not build false expectations.

3. Think in terms of **EXCEEDING CUSTOMER EXPECTATIONS**. Do what is right for the Customer... stand behind Saturn products and services. Strive to go the extra step that transforms Customer satisfaction into **CUSTOMER ENTHUSIASM**.

4. **MAKE IT HAPPEN** ... **SPEED** is essential ... Create a "**WIN-WIN**" culture and environment for the Customer, the dealer, and Saturn.

5. **FOLLOW-UP** with the Customer to ensure that the Customer's expectations were met or exceeded.

6. Seek to **CONTINUALLY IMPROVE** the quality of our products and services in the eyes of our Customers.

Exhibit 4.1   Saturn's Six Steps to Customer Enthusiasm

WHAT YOU CAN DO

Building on Core Values

- Use these Saturn values and examples as a case study. This is just one company, and it's not yours. What are *your* values? Perhaps it's time for some soul-searching.

- Plan on gathering your partners or company leaders together for an uninterrupted working session. Better make that *sessions,* because it will probably take more than one. Reserve a meeting place away from the office, maybe at some quiet, secluded retreat.

- Now think about what you want to accomplish. A new mission statement or philosophy? Core values to carry through your mission? A true commitment to creating customer loyalty? If this is new to your company, or if it's a major change, take it one step at a time—and rest assured that you will encounter some resistance. Knowing that, who will conduct the meeting? I suggest hiring an experienced facilitator to help you through the process and minimize conflict.

- Prepare your approach. Reread this chapter and the previous chapter. (Plus, you might want to first finish this book for even more ideas.) Consider each area that may need to be addressed during the session, such as the following:

    Information. The facts and figures. For example: your existing mission statement, or mission statements of other companies that you admire; facts and figures on your company's customer retention and long-term value; results of surveys or the "What You Can Do" checklist from Chapter 3; or identifying information that is missing.

    Possibilities. New ideas or alternatives. This is the time for participants to do a little creative thinking by suggesting new concepts about the company's mission, values, or customer loyalty. Suggestions should be presented in optimistic "what could be" terms. (The how and why will come later.)

Feelings. Includes hunches and intuition. Face it, chances are that not everyone will feel the same way as the leader does about each subject. Participants will need the opportunity to briefly express their likes, dislikes, or fears without having to explain reasons.

Constructive optimism and pessimism. The reasons why a suggestion may or may not work. Address the values and benefits of an idea, such as increasing customer loyalty. Logically discuss (not argue) potential problems or risks.

Now you're ready to embark upon your mission and make it happen. Before you take off, I would like to suggest one value for you to embrace throughout the process: *persistence.*

START NOW

> The mission of any business is to create and keep customers. Go back to the basics with values, and go to the top of the company. Customer loyalty starts with company leaders being enthusiastic, proud, ethical, and value-based. Then you can ask the organization to adopt those principles. And only then, finally, can you ask customers to trust you and remain loyal. It really starts with looking at yourself in the mirror and asking, "What kind of company are we?"
>
> Don't wait until it's too late, when too many customers have disappeared through the hole in the leaky bucket. Change isn't easy, and when to change isn't always evident—especially when business is good. Keep in mind these words of wisdom:
>
> "The time to repair the roof is when the sun is shining."
>
> *John F. Kennedy*

PART TWO

Before, During, and After the Purchase

Create Interest

"I Think I Want to Buy"

I had been looking for a car and talking to salespeople; I was just so distraught and confused. I was determined to do this by myself, without my husband. I thought that if I can run a business, I should be able to buy a car. One morning I noticed a car in the parking lot at the restaurant where I was meeting a group of friends for breakfast. I pointed it out to them, commenting that it was nice looking, and asked if anyone knew anything about that car. It turned out to be a Saturn. My friend Peggy spoke up and said, "My mother just bought one; my sister just bought one; it's hassle-free, you just go in there and just pay the set price." Well, that got my interest. The next day I went in there, and immediately knew that my decision was made.

Linda Bader
*(My friend, and the first Saturn
customer to create MY interest!)*

Do your customers toot their horns to others about your company's products and services? Enthusiastic, loyal customers will do that for you. And by doing so, they create interest in others.

We were attracted to Saturn for more reasons than one. It was the fun advertisements, the reputation, and referral by a family member.

Patricia Clum,
*who is now looking forward
to being a two-Saturn family*

Just as one advertisement is not enough to move a person to buy, a single method used to create interest is not enough. Saturn doesn't only rely on media advertisements or exposure. In fact, Saturn strongly believes that selling cars is a word-of-mouth business. Your decision to buy a particular make of car is shaped more by word-of-mouth opinions and referrals from family, friends, and coworkers than by advertising. The Saturn customers who told me that they were initially attracted to Saturn because of commercials or printed advertisements didn't cite those as the sole attractions. *If* customers even mentioned ads, 99 percent of the time it was in conjunction with other reasons—most commonly reputation or personal referrals.

Before we get to advertisements (which Saturn does so very well) and other means of creating interest, please understand that you must first provide *quality* products and services.

Build a Reputation through Quality and Value

I never have conversations with strangers at the gas station, but the first three times I went there with my new Saturn, everybody was asking me about it.

Maria Hutzler,
referring to her very first Saturn

When your reputation for quality is earned, people will start talking. And when they start talking, interest is created. Interest then begins attracting people to your company or product.

Everybody wants and talks quality these days, to the point where quality is expected. It just dawned on me that I'm beginning to take the quality of my Saturn for granted. After almost one year, I have not had a single problem. My point is that the necessary level of quality is being raised a notch, and a reputation for quality has to be earned. Two of Saturn's values are very evident here: "Commitment to Excel," and "Continuous Improvement," where they "seek to continually improve the quality of our products and services." And the proof is in the product: Saturn's 1997 sedan ranked first for initial quality in the annual J.D. Power and Associates survey—ahead of Toyota, Nissan, and Honda.

> *I'm an auto mechanic, and I found out they are dependable and a low-maintenance car.*
>
> John H. Stoughton,
> *who adds that "I love my Saturn."*

> *"Consumers Digest" gave it a high rating, and I like the low cost of maintenance.*
>
> Ed Scherr,
> *regarding his purchase of a used Saturn*

Saturn has been written up in lots of publications, like *Time, Motor Trend, Road & Track, Popular Mechanics*—magazines that potential customers may read and rely on for information, and share with others. Saturn cars have been selected by Intelli-Choice as "Best Overall Values of the Year." In this case, quality viewed in terms of "value" for Saturn cars includes the purchase price, overall ownership costs, and resale value. From day one, Saturn understood the importance of quality in the customer loyalty equation (see Exhibit 5.1).

Saturn's commitment to quality can also be found in their mission statement, "Market vehicles delivered and manufactured in the United States that are world leaders in quality. . . ." How well does Saturn's approach to quality work? On GM's cor-

From the Publisher

Congratulations to Saturn Corporation on the selection of six out of seven of its vehicles to the IntelliChoice list of "**Best Overall Values of the Year!**"

IntelliChoice is pleased to recognize Saturn's continued attention to value.

Since its eligibility for the award in 1993, Saturn has been a pillar of consistency year after year--and 1998 is no different. Saturn SL surpasses competitors with the lowest maintenance and insurance costs in its class. And the SW models have the best resale value among small wagons.

> "1998 marks the **sixth year in a row** a Saturn sedan has won a **"Best Overall Value,"** and the fifth year in a row the SL Series has won the **"Best Overall Value"** in their class."

That Saturn's vehicles continue to distinguish themselves is no small testament to Saturn's ongoing commitment to quality and value.

Again, congratulations on your continued success.

Peter S. Levy
President

Exhibit 5.1 IntelliChoice Publisher's Letter of Congratulations to Saturn

porate quality audits, Saturn has consistently earned the highest scores within the corporation.

Starting with a quality product sometimes means reinventing the technology and engineering better parts. For example, Saturn was the only car manufacturer to use an environmentally friendly method of casting on such a large scale to make aluminum and steel powertrain components.

Saturn started out to make a different car, with quality being a key component—like an automatic transmission that has led to today's smart automatic transmission with over 30 patents to its credit. And like Saturn's remarkable automotive innovation of dent-resistant polymer body side panels. They are two to four times more resilient than steel, are recyclable, and will fend off tree sap, ultraviolet light, nicks, dings, and corrosion (not to mention bird droppings). My Saturn is dent-free after almost one year. Recently I had to tackle the task of removing an oily-tar residue that had splashed on the car from road paving projects. I was delighted when most of it came right off during a normal wash, without having to seriously scrub or apply special cleaners.

The process of striving for quality is continuous. Saturn does it through a combination of efforts: using auto industry benchmarks, setting stringent quality goals, auditing, testing, training, and teamwork. And common sense, too, like the fact that in the design studio, the people who design the outside of the car sit right next to the people who design the interior. And both groups work very closely with the manufacturing folks, so people aren't just focusing on their own little part of the car.

The Big Three automakers collaboratively developed a quality control system called QS9000, originally for their external suppliers. Saturn members have begun implementing some of the 20 elements of this system, which covers everything from document and data control to calibrating gauges.

It's interesting to note that Saturn does not have a formal "Quality Department." Instead, they have a series of quality councils that set quality goals and provide general direction in terms of quality elements. The councils are composed of both union and management team members and meet on a periodic basis. Guess who chair the highest quality council in Saturn? None other than the president of Saturn Corporation and the president of Saturn's union local.

Saturn also has specific quality resource teams that are responsible for the development and auditing of quality procedures, quality methods, and quality systems. The quality councils and quality resource teams are in place to support the work units who are responsible for the day-to-day building of the cars and the monitoring of product quality. (A work unit is defined as an integrated group of approximately 6 to 15 team members.) Monitoring quality on a day-to-day basis is done through:

- Use of statistical methods
- Adherence to Saturn quality systems and procedures
- Appropriate use of quality-measuring and enhancement tools (charts, cause-and-effect diagrams, analyses, etc.)
- Quality-related education, including problem-solving techniques
- And, perhaps most important, inherent team motivation and enthusiasm

Since workers have a true partnership with management, they're encouraged to shape the manufacturing process themselves. In turn, it's only natural for them to care more about the product they make. Make no mistake—teamwork plays a central role. A cooperative attitude has the effect of increasing not only the number of cars produced, but more important the level of craftsmanship in each. Although robotics and computers play a large role in the manufacturing process, individual Saturn team members still have the power to stop the line at any time to correct a problem. Further, part of each team member's salary is earned by meeting stringent quality goals, which are evaluated twice quarterly by an outside auditor.

Saturn really puts cars to the test for the sake of quality. Saturn engineers patented a new way to provide traction control, something that's usually available only on far more expensive cars. To ensure that the optional antilock brakes and the traction control that goes with them work just fine, they're tested in fast stops on wet, super-slick basalt tiles. And speaking of tiles, hand-cut Belgian paving blocks that were once used to surface Chicago streets now play a role in the testing of Saturn cars. Otherwise known as "bladder blocks," they originally jolted tanks to pieces in World War II, then came to the United States as ballast on ships. From Chicago, they finally ended up at Saturn testing grounds in Milford, Michigan. To ensure a smooth ride, Saturns are driven over this punishing surface to test the chassis and suspension elements.

Saturn cars are also put through their paces in Mesa, Arizona, where temperatures can exceed 115°F for months at a time. Everything is tested, from the powertrain control module (that keeps the engine and transmission in constant communication) to the turn signal lightbulb. Remember those polymer body side panels? Well, in the desert, things deteriorate faster, so the panels and their final clearcoat flex are exposed to scorching sun there. In addition, interior vinyls, fabrics, and plastics are placed in "hot boxes," which rotate to follow the sun.

Since Saturn customers live in places other than the desert, Saturn tests the cars in other extreme environments, like up and down the steep winding roads of Pikes Peak in Colorado, in humid Florida, and in the frozen north of Kapuskasing, Canada (where winter temperatures regularly drop to −30°F). They test drive the commute traffic of Los Angeles and a 200-mile route that runs from the beaches of Ventura to the Santa Monica boardwalk.

Not all testing takes place in controlled settings. Newfoundland, Canada, is a real-life proving ground for Saturn. Conditions in St. John's combine freezing, Arctic air with briny fog and 90 tons of road salt per mile per year. The corrosion-proof polymer panels prove their value here. In January 1996, twelve Saturn owners in St. John's agreed to let Saturn install new chassis components as part of its continuous improvement philosophy. And they held up beautifully. Saturn also monitors cars with high-mileage business drivers all over the United States and Canada. A courier company in St. John's is using a Saturn wagon, and after they're done with it, Saturn will bring it back to Michigan and take it apart to see how it held up.

Quality also counts with the little things, for which Saturn brings in the SWAT team. S.W.A.T. is an acronym for Squeak and Water Audit Test team. On every shift at the plant, seven team members audit vehicles at random after they come off the production line. They attempt to experience the cars from a customer's standpoint, listening for squeaks and rattles (big aggravations for any new-car owner!) and testing for leaks. Even in the development stage of new Saturns, a "pleasability engineer" armed with a flashlight, video camera, and stethoscope pokes around in the nooks and crannies.

Continuous training is also necessary for continuous quality improvement. The goal of every team member is a minimum of 92 hours of training per year, and a portion of his or her salary is tied to meeting that goal. Some assembly team members working with specialized equipment may receive as much as 200 hours of training. An efficiency exercise is just one example of training, where a simple model car is built using inefficient methods as class members look on. They identify the types of waste they see, such as use of improper tools or excessive walking. Then they redesign the process to make it more efficient, and carry these lessons over into their own jobs.

Saturn doesn't neglect the rest of the wheel when it comes to quality. It creates Quality Achievement Awards for its suppliers. Standards are set, and suppliers who meet those standards are recognized with awards. Saturn also makes a big deal about it with a nice celebration. The enthusiasm carries over further when suppliers celebrate the awards with their own employees. As one Saturn supplier puts it, "That Saturn would recognize suppliers is a neat thing. Those opportunities (to win awards) reinforce the pride that our associates (employees) feel. We always try in the Saturn way to share that back with our organization, so we have a celebration for our 300-plus employees onsite. We give them all T-shirts with a copy of the award poster on the back of the shirt, have doughnuts, and talk. It's little things about relationships that we've learned, about the way Saturn does things with people."

Other factors count when building a reputation through quality and value. Of importance to many Saturn customers is the fact that the cars are 95 percent American-made. Safety ranks up there also, as evident from this exchange:

Last night at our CarClub meeting I met a woman taking possession of her new Saturn. (Her first was up to 134K and she was feeling a little antsy). She told me her decision to get her first Saturn was based on totaling a Plymouth. She decided then to get the safest car she could afford, and that brought her to Saturn. Now, she says she will not consider any other car. So Saturn safety does sell.

Absolutely. The reason I bought mine was because my brother fell asleep at the wheel of my parents' '92 SL1 one night. He managed to spin the car 180 degrees and T-boned with a tree, so the tree basically hit the driver's side right between the front and rear doors. He smashed hard enough to squish the driver's seat down to about eight inches wide. He walked away with a few bruises. Admittedly, he laid down on the pavement soon after, but the fact that sold me was he walked away.

Exchanges from an e-mail list of Saturn enthusiasts

One big contributor to driver and passenger safety is what Saturns have in common with million-dollar Formula 1 race cars—and what makes them different from cars of traditional unibody construction. It's the steel spaceframe—a reinforced structure that's the sturdy skeleton of every Saturn. Hidden beneath those sleek polymer panels, the Saturn spaceframe helps maintain the car's structural integrity in a crash. It's built with front and rear crumple zones, which help to absorb and isolate impact energy so less transfers to the passenger compartment. The spaceframe also makes a Saturn simpler to repair after an impact, since the polymer panels may easily be removed, and damaged sections of the spaceframe can sometimes be cut out and replaced.

It was June 14 and I was driving to work. Along comes a car with one headlight out, driven by an 18-year-old girl. She runs a red light. By the time I saw her, I couldn't even apply my brakes. When I hit her at 40 miles per hour, it knocked me out. Later, when I came to, I found out in the police report what happened. When she hit me, it knocked her car into a telephone pole, and I spun around in the opposite direction and hit the car behind me. It completely totaled my 1994 Saturn. The police said they couldn't believe I wasn't hurt worse than what I was. My air bag went off, but I still broke a little finger, tore my knee up, banged my head, and later they said I had a cracked sternum. The police told me they've heard of many people that have been in Saturns, and walked away from accidents, whereas in other cars they might not be so lucky. That sold me. I went right out and bought another Saturn.

Don Hennemann,
*almost healed two months later—
attending an owners' clinic for his
new Saturn*

The 1997 Saturn SL2 received one of the best results ever recorded by the Insurance Institute for Highway Safety in its recent low-speed crash test. The car suffered no damage in the rear-into-a-pole test, and needed just $655 in repairs for all four tests combined—the lowest since 1981 when the Ford Escort sustained no damage.

Crash tests—such as Saturn's testing of their new Reduced Force Air Bags—require months of planning. A mass of sensors collects data from both the car and its very important occupants (two Hybrid III crash dummies) and transmits it to a computer. In barrier tests, the car hurtles down a 395-foot-long corridor to collide with a reinforced concrete wall at 35 miles per hour. The dummies are each rigged with over $100,000 worth of instrumentation. Saturn is always looking out for the customers, even if the customers are real dummies.

Then came a very bad day in my life when I got in a head-on accident on a rainy wet road. The other car went out of control and we hit head-on for a combined speed of about 45 miles per hour. The air bag went, and the car went off into the ditch and up on a steel fence. I was very lucky to walk away from the accident, but the Saturn was gone. There was no hope for it, and I had to total it. To my surprise, the insurance company gave me more money for the car than I thought I was going to have to argue for. I paid $15,700 and put 82,000 miles on it. Four years later, the insurance company gave me $10,500 for the car. I couldn't believe it. They claimed the Saturns have held their value so well. It took a year before I could get myself together again to buy another car, but I can tell you this, it was another Saturn. I will continue to drive this Saturn until it will no longer work too.

"Brick,"
*from somewhere out
there on the Internet, on how
"Saturn Saved My Life"*

Accidents are unfortunate, but along with problems, they do happen. If customers have confidence in your product or service, they will keep coming back. Confidence comes from not only the quality of products and services, but also from the value they provide.

Confused about the difference between quality and value? Actually, in this situation, they are pretty much the same. Check a thesaurus for *quality,* and *value* will appear, and vice versa. Interestingly, another word that appears for *value* is the verb *appreciate.*

Saturn cars represent value. Saturn has been a pillar of consistency year after year, as its vehicles earn IntelliChoice's highest ratings in the Ownership Cost category. Resale value is but one component, for which all five models in 1997 were rated "Excellent." Not long after I purchased my Saturn, the retailer had a special four-day trade-in sale, offering 50 to 75 percent of the manufacturer's suggested retail price on one- to six-year-old Saturn trade-ins. Remember, customers like to feel that they get more than they paid for.

When you provide value for the long term, it has the added benefit of getting you through the short-term market challenges. Heed the words of Frederick F. Reichheld, author of *The Loyalty Effect:* "Creating value for customers is the foundation of every successful business system. Creating value for customers builds loyalty, and loyalty in turn builds growth, profit, and more value."[6]

Oh, yeah, just one more very important lesson on quality from Saturn: *Integrate quality into the business process with the voice of the customer.* You'll read more about how that's done in Chapter 9.

WHAT YOU CAN DO

Build a Reputation through Quality and Value

- *Benchmark.* This is measuring others' products or services according to specified standards, in order to compare with and improve your own. First, you'll need to define what is to be benchmarked. Then, document in a flowchart all the tasks or steps required in the process. For instance, if you decide to benchmark the customer ordering process, flowchart how orders are taken, entered into an order processing system, communicated to a plant, scheduled for delivery, communicated to the customer, shipped, and installed. Then, select benchmark partners who also have documented a similar process, and compare notes either once or on a regular basis. Or, you may be able to read an article about a process and compare it to your own. Benchmarking can be done with peer organizations within your company (how one sales district does against another); by comparing your performance to your competitors; or by comparing common processes across multiple firms in different industries. For example, the process of handling customer feedback might be compared from the insurance industry to industrial manufacturers. When the benchmarking is complete, adjust your standards and goals accordingly.

Here's one hint: try to build in quality and value up front. It can be more difficult to add later. Customers get weary of the "New!" and "Improved!" labels. If the first generation of Saturn cars had turned out to be junk, customers wouldn't have waited around for improved quality.

- *Review customer perceptions.* You may be surprised to learn that your customers' perceptions about quality and value are different from your own. And of course, customer perception is reality. This situation reminds me of that old black and white optical illusion picture that we studied in school. If you focused on the white, you saw a vase. If you focused on the black, you saw the profiles of two faces. Some people have been in business for so long or are so shortsighted that they only see things one way, while their customers see things in a totally different way.

Here's another way to look at this picture. The vase represents people in a company doing their jobs, and focusing exclusively on the internal, while failing to see the faces of the customers looking in at them and forming perceptions. Every employee should know who the customers are, what must be done to meet the customers' requirements, and what must be done to exceed the customers' expectations.

Find out how prospects and customers view the quality and value of what you have to offer. Discover the answer to this key question: *How many complaints and what kind of complaints do you receive that are directly related to product quality?* Review any information that you may already have, like survey results, comment cards, or calls to the service department. Talk to your customer-contact people at all levels. Talk to your customers! You'll see in subsequent chapters how Saturn is great at doing all of these things, and how you can too.

- *Compete, Share, and Celebrate.* Quality counts, whatever the size or type of your business. Fortunately, you don't have to be a 9,000-plus-employee organization like Saturn to win awards and generate articles in the press. But you should establish quality standards, and be constantly striving for new goals. Competing for quality awards is one way, and it can also help fuel the troops. Look for programs and awards offered by your industry association, manufacturers, or customers. Then, when you meet goals or win awards, share the news. Spread it to customers and employees—to all of the folks that deserve the credit for earning the award. Saturn shares news of awards with team members in various ways, like voice mail communications, over the company's internal computer system, in its daily newsletter, or through a bi-weekly video. Don't forget to let the media know. If you don't have a public relations department, hire a freelance writer to generate press releases. A nice (and free) article in the newspaper or mention on TV commands attention, and goes a lot further than a quarter-page paid advertisement or 30-second commercial. And, as you're sharing the news, don't forget to celebrate! Have a special meeting or luncheon; give out T-shirts, plaques, or an enthusiastic verbal pat on the back. Remember, rewarding positive actions increases the likelihood that the desired performance will be repeated.

Build a Reputation through Loyal Customers

I was referred by my daughter, who owns a Saturn.
Roger Burns

My brother owns a Saturn and is very satisfied.
Maureen Bunger

A coworker has one [a Saturn], and she loves hers.
James Lile

Saturn estimates that 49 percent of its customers come into Saturn retail facilities because of word-of-mouth endorsements. That's the best form of advertising available.

One of Saturn's early supporters when the cars were first launched back in 1990 was a now-deceased gentleman named Ace. He was somewhat of a legend in the San Francisco Bay area for his enthusiastic promotion of Saturn. Among other things, Ace was known for picking up brochures at the local retailer and handing them out to prospects.

Today, with all the technology available, it sometimes seems that nearly all business is done by computers, the Internet, e-mail, voice mail, fax, and telephone and the like. The truth is, nevertheless, that business is still done on a person-to-person basis.

As such, when faced with making a buying decision, we are more comfortable when a company or product has been personally recommended to us. When was the last time you looked for a doctor, or tried a different restaurant? Did a mention by a friend or coworker have any bearing on the doctor you selected? Or the restaurant you chose for dinner? So it goes with your loyal customers. They are the best spokespersons you'll ever have.

> *I know they have some type of referral program; my salesman even said he'd give me a referral fee, but I don't want to be bothered with that. I just enjoy showing off my car and telling everybody I can. I appreciate what word-of-mouth advertising has done for my business, and I'm happy to do the same for Saturn.*
>
> Linda Bader,
> *business owner and Saturn show-off*

Saturn has built a reputation through loyal customers because those loyal customers have experienced the quality and value of the cars. And they've experienced being treated right—before, during, and after their purchase. So, naturally, those thrilled customers have no qualms about telling others. When I asked customers if they had referred other people, the majority responded with a definite *Yes.* Most had directly referred one to three others, with many of those referred actually becoming new Saturn customers. And direct referrals don't include strangers who may have overheard these loyal customers bragging about their Saturns.

Saturn doesn't currently have a formal referral program that it recommends to its retailers. As long as they're done the Saturn way (incorporating Saturn philosophies and values), referral programs are really up to the retailers. Different retailers, and even individual sales consultants, have different methods for handling referrals. Take, for example, one Saturn sales consultant's description of how he's comfortable with handling referrals. Rather than asking for names of friends and family members at the time of sale, he prefers waiting until the customer has had a chance to experience the car a little bit. Asking before then, he says, "is like asking a diver, 'How's the dive?' while he's still in midair and hasn't yet hit the water." Later, in a follow-up contact, he will make sure that the customer is completely satisfied. Only then will he say to the customer something like this: "The next time you're getting out of your Saturn in a parking lot somewhere, and someone is admiring your car, I would appreciate it if you would reach into the glove compartment, retrieve one of my business cards, and pass it along. I will gladly give you $50 if that person, or any other referral, becomes one of my customers." That's $50 out of the sales consultant's pocket. Oh, he also remembers to enclose a handwritten card with the money, extending thanks for the referral.

You can see that these loyal customers like talking to others and introducing them to the Saturn way. Most Saturn retailers build on this by inviting customers to work in the Saturn exhibit area at local and regional new-car shows each year. In fact, about 50 percent of the Saturn folks at auto shows are customers! Customers tell me they look forward to and enjoy these shows. One man told me that he tries to schedule his vacation time around the show each year. After all, they get to "talk Saturn" to interested and somewhat captive audiences. They share their Saturn experiences, and many end up sparking the interest of hundreds of people at each show. Now that's a great way to build a reputation through loyal customers!

WHAT YOU CAN DO

Build a Reputation through Loyal Customers

The really enthusiastic customers don't need incentives for referring others to you. However, since those types of customers may be in the minority, there are ways you can help the process along.

- *Ask.* Many people find it difficult to ask for referrals, but the truth is that some customers just don't know or realize how much you depend on referrals. And most happy customers will be glad to help you, if you ask. Try taking it one step further than just asking, "Do you know of *anybody* . . ." For example, you operate a nature store and customer Jane Smith is an avid bird-watcher, having just purchased a fourth bird-feeder from you. You mention to Jane that members of her bird-watching club would be interested in the special new binoculars you carry that are lightweight and great for birding trips. You would be appreciative if Jane would tell all her friends at the next bird-watchers meeting. She does, and you make sales as a result. The new customers thank Jane for being a pretty smart bird. And you remember to reward Jane with a discount (at least) on her own new pair of binoculars.

- *Offer incentives.* Some customers respond better when they know they will be rewarded for referral efforts. Use your imagination, but make sure that you also employ a healthy dose of ethics. Don't violate any laws or company policies. The incentives you choose don't have to be the same for every customer. One may appreciate a gift certificate to a fine restaurant; another may like a box of chocolates. Others may prefer cold, hard cash. Other incentives to consider include anything free (your product or a weekend getaway trip), or a reduced price on the customer's next purchase. The level or cost of the incentive should of course be in line with the value of the referrals that you receive. Our local automobile association had a referral contest, with drawings for different gifts based on the number of referrals each member submitted. Gifts ranged from key chains up to vacation packages—which leads to my next point.

- *Acknowledge referrals.* At a minimum, acknowledge referrals by sending a thank-you note. People like to know that their efforts are appreciated, and they may even respond by sending you more referrals! A retirement and financial planner tells me her company receives lots of referrals, so many that it can be difficult to keep up with them. When they do catch up on sending thank-you-for-your-referral letters, they end up getting dozens of additional referrals in return!

- *Make it easy for customers to refer.* Some customers may be comfortable with passing along your business card or a brochure. Others won't mind completing a referral form. If you're requesting someone to complete and return a referral form, provide a self-addressed, stamped envelope or toll-free fax number. When a customer gives you a referral, clarify contact or follow-up expectations, like who calls whom. Keep customers informed of new products or services, or changes, so that they can speak knowledgeably for you. You could also suggest to your customers a particular type of company or person—within their circle of influence—that would benefit from what you offer.

- *Keep track.* When dealing with a large number of customers and referrals, it is necessary to have some type of tracking system. Whether you write on an index card or enter data in a computer, record who your referrals are coming from and who's being referred. Include notes on any acknowledgement sent or action required and taken, like sending a thank-you note, making contact with the referred prospect, sending a follow-up letter, or scheduling a future appointment. Then be sure to review the information on a regular basis. A customer who has referred ten new clients to you over the past year should warrant a higher level of recognition than a customer who has referred one. (Just think of the money saved on the cost of acquiring those ten new clients, and the revenue you've gained as a result!) You'll also want to monitor the referral system to learn whether the chosen methods are effective, or if it's time for a change. Maybe your customers just aren't influenced by a cash offer. Or maybe you can no longer keep up with writing on index cards. If something's not working, change your approach!

Create Interest by Being Different!

Saturn: "a different kind of company; a different kind of car." Okay, so how do they go about creating interest by being different? I think it shows in five areas, which we'll look at in more detail in this section:

1. Advertisements
2. Open Doors
3. Show Me
4. Unexpected Placement
5. Electronically Speaking

Advertisements

The voice-over says, "We kept our new coupe a secret before we introduced it to the public. We covered up the name so that you'd be surprised when you finally saw it in the showroom." Meanwhile, the TV commercial is showing a guy getting out of a car and entering a small-town diner. His car has no identifying name or logo; they're covered up. The rest of the commercial goes like this:

Another man at the counter asks, "Whose red car is that out there in the parking lot?"

"It's mine; am I blocking you?" responds the driver.

"No, it kinda caught my eye when I walked by. So, what is it?"

As the driver gets up to leave—putting on his jacket with the Saturn name and logo all over it—he replies "I'm not supposed to tell you."

The voice-over cuts in again with, "We never thought, though, that people would be able to figure out what car it was just by meeting the people that test-drove it."

That is just one of many fine Saturn commercials that have, I believe, had a significant role in creating interest in the car. Saturn's TV commercials have from the very beginning represented another way that Saturn is different. Just mention Saturn commercials to any adults who watch TV, and I'll bet they won't hesitate to tell you about *their* favorite Saturn commercial.

Advertising plays a big part in brand management, which is the craft of building a brand's image and value in the public eye. Saturn is the best auto brand manager, according to a 1998 *Automotive News* survey of 100 brand managers and marketing executives at auto manufacturers and their advertising agencies. Saturn even topped luxury automakers Mercedes-Benz, Lexus, and BMW. Some large corporations with many different brands, like Proctor & Gamble, have annual internal advertising awards for which brand teams compete. In 1997, for the first time, Saturn competed in GM's internal award program. Seven marketing divisions with about 35 different brands competed for nine Alpha Awards. Saturn took home three out of those nine Alpha awards.

Saturn is great at using real customer stories in their commercials. The very first Saturn customer to act out her story before a camera was Robin Millage. Back in 1990, Robin lived on a tiny island in Alaska, where she provided cab service. She saw Saturn ads, and thought the cars looked reliable. But there was one little problem: There were no Saturn retail facilities in Alaska at that time. The nearest retailer was in Seattle—500 miles away. So, what did Robin do? She ordered a new Saturn, *sight unseen,* from the Seattle facility. Later, when Robin's car required the repair of a seat-back recliner mechanism (and with no retailer nearby), a Saturn technician traveled 4,000 miles—from Spring Hill, Tennessee to Alaska—to make the repair. That commercial almost wasn't produced because of concern that it would seem far-fetched. The fact is that about 97 percent of all Saturn advertising involves real-life stories, although sometimes actors portray the real customers. One interesting thing about Robin's story is how it found its way to be used in advertising. The actual event happened very quietly. A team member at Saturn's Customer Assistance Center in Spring Hill learned of Robin's repair situation from a call to their 800 number. Naturally (to Saturn), the right thing to do was to send somebody up to repair the car, so they did. There was no fanfare, and the episode was almost forgotten. Then along came a diligent writer from Saturn's ad agency, researching some stories for use in Saturn's brochure. Only then was the story told to the rest of the world.

Saturn's commercials and other advertisements have a way of connecting with our basic, good values, while creating interest. An article in *USA Today*[7] quipped that "Saturn has been churning out ads that are the commercial equivalent of a favorite pair of blue jeans: comfortable, reliable, personal."

From the beginning, Saturn's advertising philosophy has been to take the high road, to be different from typical car advertising. You know what I mean—a car hugging a wet mountain road, a truck kicking up dirt, screams of "buy now!" and "don't miss the giant sale-a-thon!" or just showing the car. Saturn's ads are more subtle. They're focused on people, both customers and team members, from the plant to the retail facilities. They indirectly talk about aspects of personal values and car quality.

Does this advertising mean that Saturn neglects its loyal customers, while focusing on potential new customers? To the contrary. According to a Saturn marketing team member, "Our advertising not only needs to speak to potential new customers, but we also always want to speak to our existing customers. We try to make them feel good about what they bought and about the company that they do business with, and to enjoy the ownership experience. The experience goes beyond just buying a car; it's about owning a car, and owning the next car."

Another thing that makes Saturn's advertising unique is that a consistent message appears at local, regional, and national levels. The company's "market area approach" (selecting only one retailer for a given geographical area) keeps retailers from competing directly with one another. This means harmony in advertising on the different levels. Retailers do have standard guidelines to follow for their local advertising, which is generally in newspaper and on the radio, although some larger retailers also do TV advertising. Retailers also participate on marketing councils that approve creative direction for regional work. And while many companies have different ad agencies at regional and national levels, Saturn has stuck with only Hal Riney & Partners since the beginning. This "one-voice philosophy" gives a consistent look and feel to the ads, so customers hear the same thing at all three levels.

I'd like to share a few examples of Saturn TV commercials that I think help create interest. One commercial features a woman toll booth operator, holding up piles of traffic, asking people how they like their Saturn. Then she says, "I must have talked to at least two to three thousand different Saturn owners. Every single one of them absolutely love their car!"

Another commercial follows a husband and wife who are driving around town, passing and waving at relatives in their different Saturns as they go about their daily routines. Seems there are nine Saturns in the family!

Then there's a lady in a full clown outfit, driving around with a Saturn full of stuffed animals. She says it "lifts peoples' spirits. People are always looking at this car!"

WHAT YOU CAN DO

Advertisements

- Of course, advertisements alone are not going to create loyal customers. Remember that ads are just one more marketing tool, and strive to create interest and new customers through word of mouth.

- Any advertising campaign needs to begin with a strategy and goals, so that's where you start. If the strategy is to create interest, the messages that you're sending should connect with the company values and your customers' values in some way, and reinforce loyal customers' feelings when they see or hear your messages.

- Check your various advertising methods for consistency in image, and for accuracy and completeness. A specialty clothing store ran an ad in Louisville's newspaper recently. It was a nice, big, expensive quarter-page ad. There was no location map, but there was a street address. Anybody in Louisville reading the ad would have had a very hard time finding that street or the store, because it was in Lexington—60 miles away! I doubt that potential customers would be interested enough to take the time to figure it out.

- Creating interest by being different through advertising sometimes means looking outside what your industry normally does. Some Saturn retailers use the testimony of loyal customers in their local commercials. This is generally a good deal all the way around. People that aren't your customers—but who recognize or know the customers in the commercial—are now interested in your customer's experience. Plus, those customers talk. They tell other people to watch or listen for them on the commercial. The bigger picture is that people would rather do business with someone who has been recommended to them. Enthusiastic customers in commercials are effective in making those recommendations for you.

Open Doors

Driving along I-65 in Tennessee, just south of Nashville, you'll notice an exit for Saturn Parkway, which takes you over to Highway 31 and Spring Hill. What you won't notice from Highway 31 is the Saturn plant. It was designed to blend in with and preserve the surrounding countryside. As you follow the signs to the Welcome Center and wonder where the heck it is, you'll see a horse barn. Surprise, the welcome center *is* the horse barn! Actually, the barn, built of native limestone, was formerly the home of Tennessee walking horses, including one grand champion. It has been refurbished and turned into a 10,000-square-foot interactive exhibition center, filled with every aspect of Saturn's story, as well as the history of the horse farm. Here you can do things like:

- Arrange to go on a group tour of the plant
- Participate in the Saturn experience, as letters from enthusiastic customers come to life in an interactive kiosk
- Learn about "the spirit of Saturn—teamwork"
- Sample what Saturn does in the communities across the country

- Learn about Saturn's role in helping to preserve the environment
- Learn a little about the manufacturing process

One of my favorites is an interactive display of Saturn's famous polymer panels. At the touch of a button, a shopping cart rolls downhill, into a polymer door panel, BANG!, and leaves no dents!

> *I toured the Spring Hill plant with my wife and two kids. I was quite impressed with the streamlined operation. We were led right by some of the workstations and the workers were very reactive to our presence. They had numerous signs up welcoming us and thanking us for having bought Saturns. They also weren't hesitant to return our waves and smiles. It was an uplifting experience for me and made me even more proud to be a Saturn owner. It was great to have had a chance to see exactly how my car was made. I also got a chance to see up close the newly designed models, which were just beginning to be built. It was better than looking at them on the dealership lot!*
>
> Bill Kirkpatrick,
> *who toured the plant during*
> *the 1994 Homecoming*

Plant tours are a biggie. Especially when people can see dedicated, friendly workers, and well-maintained facilities. One Saturn commercial showed a tram loaded with smiling, camera-bearing folks touring the plant in Spring Hill. It was likened to an amusement park experience, complete with a carnival barker. Fun *and* interesting. A service manager for a Saturn retail facility describes his "interesting" experience:

> I was supposed to have toured the plant with a group, but at the time, the plant had shut down for a couple of hours because the foundry had a problem. Nonetheless, I went back to the training class and expressed how enthusiastic I was about seeing the plant

in operation. The next day, there is a knock at the door. "Hey you, come with me," a friendly voice said. We hopped in a car and drove to the main entrance of the plant. There we donned hard hats and walked the plant for several hours. I put on tires; I shook hands with fellow teammates; I saw Inspiration Point, which is not an attraction on the group tour. I was like a kid in a candy store. There were bake sales in the plant; mail being delivered on three-wheeled bikes. I saw a preproduction coupe. The inside of the plant is like walking into a showroom, spotless and organized. When you take this tour, you will understand why Saturn is not just a car, but a way of life.

Saturn has created an informative and welcoming facility that customers will visit. And who do you suppose visits besides customers? Friends and relatives of fellow travelers. Lots of tour groups. Lots of PEOPLE—a big base of potential NEW CUS-TOMERS. Recent figures show that, on the average, 1,200 people per week visit the new Welcome Center!

WHAT YOU CAN DO

Open Doors

- Are your business doors open to customers and prospects? Interest and excitement can be created by letting people experience your company, process, products, and services. They'll feel connected, like part of the process. On the other hand, closed doors and lack of information may create interest—of the wrong kind. Along the lines of, "What do you have to hide?"

- No, you don't have to build a 10,000-square-foot welcome center or offer daily plant tours, but you get the idea. Opening doors to create interest doesn't have to be difficult to do, or expensive. For example, a stoneware company in Louisville has a retail shop under the same roof as the manufacturing plant. Curious shoppers can see the artists in action, and take a short self-guided tour of the process. There is one area set aside where customers are invited to paint their own designs. If that doesn't work for your business, maybe an occasional open house celebration will do. Or, here's another idea. At the offices of a consulting firm where I once worked, we had a "Client Hall of Fame." Hung on the walls were proudly displayed framed items associated with some of our major clients and their products, like a model truck, a jar of polymer, and an empty bag bearing a product identification and logo. The "Hall" created a sense of pride when clients saw it, and it created interest (and invited stories) when potential clients saw it.

Show Me

We like the dissected car in the showroom.

James and Adele Lile

Many Saturn retailers have a cutaway of a real car in the showroom (see Exhibit 5.2). Needless to say, it arouses curiosity, and you can't help being interested. It also makes it easy for the sales consultant to address any concern or question about the car. Small explanation signs at each key point help tell the story. Features and benefits are easily explained because you can *see* them, and *touch* them. Reinforced steel space frame. An air bag that's been deployed. An engine designed for easy servicing. Door panels that bounce back from a hit. It really made an impression on me when I could see some of these features. Talk about different—I didn't kick the tires, but I did get to kick the door panel and watch it bounce back unscathed!

Exhibit 5.2   Saturn Cutaway Car

A customer told me about one retailer out west that displayed in the showroom an actual crashed and crumpled, thoroughly wrecked Saturn. The story behind it is that, amazingly, the customer survived the wreck just fine and promptly purchased another Saturn. What better way to make a point about safety features?

WHAT YOU CAN DO

Show Me

- People like to have something they can see, touch, feel, hold, smell, hear, taste, and otherwise experience with their senses. Provide samples or demonstrations of your product to create customer interest. Did you ever go to a grocery store on a Saturday afternoon when they're offering free samples? Sometimes you can sample your way through a full course meal! Here's the premise: If you try it, you'll like it. If you like it, you'll buy it.

- If you sell a service or product that's difficult to demonstrate, opt for photos, videos, or testimonial stories from customers. Consider using some of the great new technologies for computer presentations. Paint a picture that people can see and experience!

Unexpected Placement

It was really unexpected, seeing a car store in the mall. I probably wouldn't have thought of Saturn, but I was already there doing other shopping. I could browse at my convenience and pick up literature.

Surprised mall shopper

Saturn of Louisville tried a different approach at creating interest by leasing a storefront in a mall. It was just a temporary arrangement for about six months, until another tenant was found. The satellite showroom had six to eight cars on display. One person staffed the store, only to answer questions when asked. It was strictly for show—there was no selling, nothing to buy. Folks could browse, examine the cars, pick up brochures, get information, or schedule a test-drive at the real facility. The thinking was that people who wouldn't normally visit the car lot would see and visit the mall store. And hopefully, interest would be created for people to then visit the lot. It worked. The retailer estimated that the mall store resulted in selling eight additional cars per month.

I remember being surprised at seeing a really giant Saturn going down the road several years ago. Actually, it was a city bus, *totally* painted to look like a Saturn. Saturn of Louisville was the first company in town to try this new type of traveling billboard.

Saturn showrooms typically have an area that displays "Saturn stuff" for sale. Things like shirts, caps, sweaters, jackets, umbrellas, beach towels, golf balls, cookie jars, coffee mugs, oven mitts, flashlights, clocks, key chains, coolers, playing cards, sunglasses, shoe-shine kits, pen-and-pencil sets, baby bibs, sand pails, coloring books . . . well, I think you get the picture. At the Welcome Center in Spring Hill, Tennessee, there's a whole shop full of this stuff. Of course, all of this "stuff" displays the Saturn logo. Customers buy this stuff for themselves and as gifts for others. So you never know where you might see the Saturn logo, and what interest it might create.

WHAT YOU CAN DO

Unexpected Placement

- Consider placing your product for sale or display, or a description of your services, in an unexpected place. Maybe you could partner with another business whose customers would have a related interest. I saw brochures advertising a pet-sitter at my veterinarian's office. There's a combination TCBY Yogurt and Blimpie Sub shop nearby, and the owner told me about another location that combined those two with a gas station. (They get your business morning, noon, and night!) One real success story is a two-person music production company in Louisville that managed to get their CDs packaged with a major perfume line. The title and theme of the CD were a great match with the name and image of the perfume. It was value-added for the customer, and great exposure for the music company.

Electronically Speaking

In the past few years, you've probably encountered the growing "message-on-hold" industry. You phone a business, get placed on hold, and instead of hearing silence or boring elevator music, you hear some type of message. Now, have you ever been so interested in hearing that message that when the person picks up to answer—interrupting the message—you ask to be *put back on hold* so you can hear rest of the message? It happens occasionally, especially if something has sparked your interest. Some Saturn retailers wisely use this opportunity of a captive audience to create interest, in perhaps a roundabout way. Their messages tend to cover a variety of topics. They announce the date and a few details about the next new-car owners' clinic; tell about new models or the computerized vehicle selection system; offer maintenance tips; announce community events; give service hours; offer information about the Saturn CarClub, or in some way provide something that may capture the interest of callers.

Saturn's web site (http://www.saturn.com) offers a variety of things that create interest for both prospects and customers. You can find the nearest retailer along with a location map, order a brochure, and get answers to FAQs (frequently asked questions). Visit the interactive pricing center, and you can build your own Saturn, calculate a monthly payment, apply for credit preapproval, or find out about leasing. You can talk to Saturn, learn about the CarClub, order Saturn stuff, and do or see lots of other things that create interest.

Saturn rightly considers the e-mail connection a very important part of its web site. The company receives between 2,000 and 2,500 e-mail messages each month. Every single one receives a response. A staff of 9 to 10 people at Saturn handles the e-mail (in addition to other things). And get this—they respond within 24 hours! (Wouldn't it be wonderful if all businesses followed this lead?!) Approximately 53 percent are requests for information or suggestions—proof that interest is being created.

Does it pay off? Saturn received an e-mail thank-you from a customer, noting that she had been "about two days away" from purchasing a competitor's car, when the information available through Saturn's web site sold her on a Saturn. And a Saturn retail facility in Georgia tracked about six car sales in one month that were related to customers getting information from their web site.

WHAT YOU CAN DO

Electronically Speaking

- Check out a message-on-hold system for your business. Avoid the tendency to create a commercial with your message. Think instead of providing information that might spark the callers' interest.

- When it comes to the Internet and web sites, the real trick (again) is to make information available that will create interest. It has to be more than just a brochure. Yes, you can and should fill it full of information. But the more interactive your site is, the better. Have a question of the week and let people post their responses to share with others. Offer the ability to shop or obtain a quote on-line. Give e-mail addresses and links. Have contests that introduce prospects to your products and services. Your site should include things that not only create initial interest for prospects, but also create ongoing interest for customers. Give customers the opportunity to talk with each other or to share their experiences using your product. Keep in mind that a web site is not *the* one and only answer, but it can be one more tool in a toolbox full of "things that create interest."

- Seek out other electronic options that will help you create interest—preferably ones that may actually make your job easier. Fax-on-demand systems are one such option.

Although not for every business, these systems are now popular and even affordable for small businesses. The beauty of these systems is that prospects or customers can access information at their convenience, and it's all done by computer. Fax-on-demand systems allow a caller to punch in a document number for their request, enter their fax machine number, then hang up. Almost immediately, the caller's fax machine is receiving the requested document. A state-wide membership association utilizes their fax-on-demand system to make available membership information and benefits, opportunities for continuing education, student information, and legislation information. Several years ago, I had a problem with my fax machine late one evening (the only time, other than weekends, when problems occur), and of course there was no one available to answer the manufacturer's customer assistance line. But, a recorded message did direct me to their fax-on-demand system. I naturally punched in the document number for "problems and solutions," received the document right away, and fixed my machine within minutes. Then, with my interest having been captured by other available documents, I couldn't resist ordering one to learn about the manufacturer's new and improved fax machines (i.e., possible future sales for the company!).

EARN INTEREST

Find out from customers how they heard about you, what created their interest, and what their perception of your business is. Build on what you learn, and then improve on that. Earn a reputation for quality products and services by providing value, through your loyal customers, and by being different. Communicate news of company awards, and celebrate with all

(Continues)

(Continued)

the people whose hard work contributed to winning those awards. Encourage referrals, and find an appropriate way to thank and reward customers for providing those referrals. Create interest by being different. Create excitement and loyal customers, and you will be sparking the interest of others—in other words, creating future customers!

6

Help Customers Feel Welcome

"I'm Ready to Visit"

When I first walked in the showroom door, there was this lady right there, and she acted like she was really glad I was there. It was like when you come to my house for dinner, and I'm waiting for you and greeting you at the door.

Then the woman introduced me to a salesperson. It was like she was introducing her brother! I already felt like, well, I'm in the Saturn family now.

Linda Bader,
continuing to tell her Saturn experience

Welcome to the Saturn family.

What happens the first time a potential customer calls or visits your business? No matter how great your products or services really are, if the first few seconds of that initial contact don't make a person feel welcome, they just might choose NOT to put that other foot in the door.

The word *Welcome* should conjure up feelings consistent with adjectives like nice, pleasant, agreeable, and favorable.

We're talking some pretty basic stuff here about dealing with people, so this not a particularly lengthy chapter. However, that doesn't mean it's not important. This should merit your full attention. It's classic Saturn when it comes down to treating people right. This is all part of the Saturn process that was designed to change the way cars are sold. Saturn recognizes the significance of *each* contact with a customer or potential customer. Focusing on the customer is what sets Saturn apart from the competition, and focusing on basic customer contact skills is part of the key to success.

Saturn recognizes how challenging it can be to consistently interact with customers in a Saturn-like way, particularly in the hectic, high-paced environment of a retail facility. That's one reason why they offer retail facility team members a 1.5-day course on customer contact skills. The primary focus of the course is to ensure that retail members understand the critical role they play as individuals toward creating customer enthusiasm. (And remember, customer enthusiasm leads to customer loyalty.) The course is designed to equip retail team members with the skills and tools necessary to exceed customers' expectations. Upon completing the course, participants should be able to:

- Identify and apply customer contact skills
- Accurately assess customer communication styles, and respond appropriately
- Manage challenging customer interactions and situations
- Learn effective listening skills
- Use professional telephone procedures and etiquette
- Respond to and refer customer inquiries efficiently and accurately

As explained in the course overview, "Examining the effect our actions have on customers will help ensure we take Saturn to the next level of excellence and gain lifetime customers. In today's world, leaving your team members' customer contact skills to chance just doesn't make good business sense. And given ever-increasing competition, it's a chance we can't afford to take." It's been my experience that too many businesses do leave these skills to chance—and that's a mistake.

The Golden Rules

Remember the Golden Rule that we learned as children? Once upon a time, a pastor asked during the children's sermon if anyone knew the Golden Rule. One young fellow volunteered, "Those who have the gold make the rules." Customers have the gold, so they get to make the rules. Every business person should practice the following variation of the Golden Rule, which is inherent in Saturn's values:

> Treat each customer the way
> YOU want to be treated as a customer.

Customers have some pretty basic needs in common, and one of those basic needs is to feel welcome. Think about the time when your phone call to a place of business was finally answered on the tenth ring—by a person whose gruff hello made you feel like a very unwelcome intruder. Or the time when a store clerk ignored you and took off in the opposite direction. Did you feel welcome? One warehouse-type home and garden center ran a cute TV commercial mocking the competition, where clerks ignored customers and brushed off a plea for help with the response, "That's not my department." But I didn't find it funny when I tried to shop at that store (the one promoting its helpful clerks) and couldn't even FIND a clerk.

My daughter (a Saturn owner) told me to go to Saturn when I was looking for a new car. The salesman pointed at the coupes and said, "There they are. I won't bother you again. I'll just tell you one thing: the price on the sticker is the price you pay." He was nice and straightforward, and that was exactly how I wanted to be treated.

Roger Burns

Which brings to mind another variation of the Golden Rule, one found within Saturn's "Customer Philosophy" (Chapter 3):

Above all else, treat Customers the way they wish to be treated.

Customers are individuals, with individual preferences. Concentrate on developing that one-to-one relationship, and learn about each customer's unique situation and wants. It is not about how *you* want it. For example, on Mary Chism's second Saturn purchase, she told her sales consultant that she just wasn't comfortable being treated to the usual Saturn send-off (you'll read about the send-off in Chapter 8). He complied with her wishes, but still wanted to show some appreciation. Later, Mary discovered a gift certificate for her favorite restaurant that her sales consultant had placed in her car.

Keeping in mind these Golden Rules, let's look at four ways that Saturn does—and you can—help customers feel welcome:

1. On the phone

2. In writing

3. In person

4. With the business appearance

On the Phone

Now that I think about it, I realize that when I have called Saturn retailers, my phone calls were handled very professionally. Once when I phoned for a sales consultant, the receptionist was able to tell me right away that he wasn't due in until later, but offered to take a message or connect me with voice mail, or to find someone else to help me. It was nice to have a choice. And it was nice to be greeted in a friendly tone of voice.

Responding to inquiries is an important part of helping potential customers feel welcome. Saturn provides a toll-free phone number (800-522-5000) for potential buyer inquiries. Typically, about 2,500 "legitimate prospect" calls per month come into this line from people requesting brochures or information on the closest retail facility. The 800 line receives an additional 3,500 to 4,000 calls per month from people just asking basic questions, or calls that need to be connected to the customer assistance center. Incoming calls are handled through a sophisticated and automated phone system, and callers hear a very pleasant recorded greeting asking them to please hold for a Saturn team member who will help with their request. Goals are for each call to be answered within 40 seconds, but the clock starts ticking the very second that a call comes in (at the start of the greeting). Most callers are talking to a real person within 13 to 20 seconds.

The task of answering these calls used to be outsourced, but is now handled in-house at Saturn by 9 to 10 people. These team members do not follow a script when answering the phone; each person develops his or her own style. True to the "Saturn family" image, they're friendly, helpful, and personable. They are hired for "people skills" in the Saturn way. Then they are trained for four weeks, in four areas: product knowledge and the phone system; technical issues; systems; and procedural issues, like who handles what. This combination of systems and skilled and trained people produces a great welcoming for potential customers.

WHAT YOU CAN DO

On the Phone

Check out your own business phone system—from the outside. If *you* have trouble negotiating the system, just imagine what problems customers or prospects are encountering. Don't count on them to be patient and forgiving. Remember that your goal is to make callers feel welcome. So, pretend that you're a customer and call your place of business. Observe what *really* happens, not what you believe should happen. Take notes as you search for answers to these questions:

- Was the phone answered promptly?
- Did you receive a friendly greeting?
- Did you get transferred around needlessly?
- Did you have trouble keeping up with all the instructions that the automated attendant went on and on and on about?
- Did you wait on hold for a long time—in silence?
- Are voice mail messages current? ("Hi, this is Susie. I'll be out of the office until October 1." That's nice to know—but not if the current date is October 10!)
- Does your system, or do your people, play "pass the customer"?

Here's one especially frustrating version of "pass the customer" that perhaps you've experienced yourself: being sucked into the black void of automated telephone attendants and voice mail. You know, when a computer answers the phone, and you can't ever connect with a REAL person? A friend recently phoned a company long distance to find out where his local representative was located. After listening to a long menu presented by an automated attendant, and making several selections, each time he ended up with some individual's voice mail. Finally, he got back to the main menu, where you supposedly could be connected to the receptionist by pressing 0. Of course, you know what happened. He got the receptionist's voice mail message! Another person told me of a similar experience, when she was trying to reach a colleague at a client's office. She suffered through this voice mail runaround for an entire day—without ever talking to a real person or locating her colleague.

Maybe you're a very busy one-person company, on the phone all the time. You really don't need, or can't afford, all that fancy phone equipment. That's no excuse to let prospects or customers who are trying to call you encounter a busy signal. More new phone services are becoming available almost every day—including one option that eliminates busy signals. If you are on the phone taking that million-dollar order, the new customer trying to call hears a short ring, then gets your voice mail. The customer hears your voice politely explain something like, "I'm on another call at the moment, but if you leave a message, I will return your call within twenty minutes." (Then deliver on your promise.)

Make sure that the people answering incoming calls for your business:

- Possess friendly people skills
- Understand the importance of customers
- Receive appropriate training on the equipment and systems

Try this before you answer the phone next time (and it doesn't matter if you're the receptionist or CEO): force yourself to smile

BEFORE you pick up the phone. Doing so really can carry over in your voice and in your attitude. Over the phone, the tone of your voice makes a huge impact. Some telemarketers are advised to keep a mirror on their desk, and to glance in it frequently to make sure they're smiling. Also, be sure to answer the phone promptly (no more than three rings) and be courteous. It doesn't cost you anything to be courteous, but you sure could lose a lot by not being courteous!

Regarding the phone, many Saturn retailers have their own 800 numbers for the convenience of customers. If you wish to attract customers from a distance, help them feel welcome with your own toll-free number.

In Writing

Back before I was a Saturn customer, I called their toll-free number, seeking information. I received answers over the phone, and these were soon followed by more information in the mail. There was a friendly cover letter, one that made me feel welcome (See Exhibit 6.1).

On the back of the cover letter was complete "1997 Saturn Suggested Retail Pricing" information. Attached to the letter were full-page road maps locating three Saturn retailers in my part of the state. A brochure showing the cars was also enclosed.

Here are a few observations about this information that I received in writing:

- It was easy to read.

- It was complete—providing the information I needed, but not overwhelming me with unnecessary fluff.

Saturn Information Team
P.O. Box 3900
Peoria, IL 61612
Telephone (800) 522-5000

Ms. Vicki Lenz

Dear Ms. Lenz:

So, the guy you take your coffee breaks with at work just bought a Saturn. Or, your neighbor drives one. Or maybe you just heard our name mentioned in conversation. In any case, you were curious enough to contact us. And we're glad you did.

As you may know, well over a million cars ago the very first Saturn rolled off the assembly line in Spring Hill, Tennessee. In the years that followed, we've done some other things you might find kind of interesting. We've enclosed a brochure that'll tell you more about us.

Once you've had the chance to look things over, please feel free to stop by one of our Saturn retailers for a test-drive and to meet our local team members. While you're there, ask about our CarCare Clinics, Used Cars from Saturn and CarClub. (It'll give you a good idea of what we're about.)

And thanks again for your interest. We hope you find just what you're looking for.

Sincerely,

Saturn Information Team

Saturn retailer(s) near you include: Saturn Of Louisville, KY.
Saturn Of Lexington, KY.
Saturn Of Florence, KY.

P.S. the SL2 is currently available in red and straight black, and the SL1, SC1 and SC2 in straight black.

enclosure

Exhibit 6.1 Letter from Saturn Information Team

- It sparked my interest and gave me the feeling that I would indeed be welcome at a Saturn retail facility.

- It provided current and accurate information.

- It made it easy for me to take the next step in the buying process.

- I was thanked for my interest.

These letters and brochures are mailed out by the same team members who answer the toll-free incoming calls. The requested information is mailed within 24 to 48 hours (unless it's a weekend). What Saturn considers as reasonable response time would put many other companies to shame. Yet, quick response not only makes potential customers feel welcome—it is expected.

WHAT YOU CAN DO

In Writing

Set prompt turnaround standards for responding in writing to inquiries. Remember to base them on your *customers'* expectations—not when *you* feel like doing it.

Review whatever it is that you send out in writing. Then, reiterating my observations of what I received in writing from Saturn, ensure that what you send is:

- Easy for an uninitiated newcomer to understand

- Complete, but not burdensome

- Inviting

- Current and accurate

- Appreciative

In Person

At Saturn, everyone was friendly. I didn't feel preyed upon or neglected.

Lesia Bennett,
expressing roughly the same sentiment
of many other Saturn customers

Some people weren't quite so kind when describing to me their experiences at those *other* auto dealerships. You know what I mean—the word "vulture" was used several times. You're pounced on by aggressive salespeople the moment you set foot in the parking lot. Instead of being made to feel welcome, you feel like a cornered mouse, at their mercy. Now, why is this? Chances are about 85 percent that you will not buy on the first visit. Yet salespeople tend to put forth a 100 percent effort to *make* you buy on that first visit. So if you're hounded 100 percent on that first visit and don't buy, how warm a welcome will you expect the second or third time?

You are welcomed as a friend at Saturn retailers, in their famous "no-hassle" manner. (What we're talking about in this chapter is the initial welcoming process. The next chapter will explain all about the no-hassle, no-haggle sales approach.) As one team member describes it, "People want to be treated fairly. This is especially true in the automotive industry where expectation levels used to be at an all-time low." He further prescribes his own version of the Golden Rule, "I treat people the way I would want my mother to be treated."

If you choose to browse the lot for two hours at a Saturn facility without a sales consultant tagging along—no problem. Or, if you do want their help—no problem. When you first walk in the showroom door at many Saturn facilities, you are welcomed by an official greeter. Their job is to make you feel welcome. I noticed an item in Saturn of Louisville's newsletter announcing "an opportunity for Saturn owners!" The opportunity presented was this: "If you find yourself easily bragging about Saturn, why not get paid for it? Saturn of Louisville is looking for part-time greeters and product specialists to greet guests and inform them about our quality lineup of models." This practice is fairly typical at Saturn retail facilities.

The greeting that people receive as they enter a Saturn showroom is friendly and helpful, just like Linda's experience at the beginning of this chapter: ". . . she (the greeter) acted like she was really glad I was there. It was like when you come to my house for dinner, and I'm waiting for you and greeting you at the door." My understanding of the importance of this simple step was reawakened recently when I visited my bank. It's a small, local bank that I had switched my business account to, looking for that friendly neighbor-type service. And it was that way—in the beginning. Everybody in the place would enthusiastically give you a welcoming greeting the moment you walked in the door . . . until a few weeks ago. As I stood in the open lobby waiting to meet with any one of the bank's office workers or officials, I was in full view—yet totally ignored—by no fewer than *seven* of those people. They were too busy talking to each other or doing paperwork. I was the only customer standing there, obviously looking for help! Yet, there was no eye contact, no hand wave, or any type of acknowledgment that I existed. All it would have taken was for any one of those people to look at me and say, "Someone will be right with you."

There are numerous ways that Saturn people help customers feel welcome in person, and customers say it best. So, I'm going to share with you some of the responses I received from Saturn customers in answer to this question:

When you visited a Saturn showroom for the first time, what was your impression of the way you were greeted, or the way you were treated?

Friendly, but not pushy—they usually let you make the first move. I was pleasantly surprised when I was offered something to drink and one of those wonderful cookies! I like the idea of being able to browse on the lot without being hounded by someone. I was treated with great respect and consideration.

Pat Garrity

We were well received—with courtesy and respect. We were treated as friends.

Ed Champa

I was treated like I was the only customer that mattered.

Mary Lou Carver

I was greeted promptly. I also noticed that the salespeople were dressed in casual slacks and golf shirts with the Saturn name and logo. It made us feel comfortable since we were dressed in shorts and T-shirts. They also had on name badges, which I appreciated since I have a hard time remembering names.

Lynn Smith

I felt wanted and welcome, and comfortable.

Leona Case

Everyone who works there seems happy. The sales staff and receptionist impressed me. I am a receptionist myself, so I notice things like sincerity when talking to someone and being helpful. More people need to be like that. When I went to get a soft drink, it was purchased for me, and I was offered fresh cookies. I was introduced to a salesman (as if I was important—really important).

Patti Clum

I was greeted promptly, with smiles. I was treated like I wasn't stupid; they showed interest.

John Stoughton

I was treated like I was family, not just a stranger.

Maureen Bunger

I was approached in the parking lot, with a handshake. There was no pressuring. I am not experienced in buying cars or [in] the features of cars. I was not treated like I was unexperienced, nor was I treated like I was stupid. They believe no question is a stupid question.

Maria Hutzler

Saturn treated us like we were their ONLY customers (and they still do!).

Linda and David Umbenhen

As a single female, I took my dad along so I wouldn't be harassed by an aggressive salesperson. This was unnecessary. They treated me very nicely and spoke to ME, not my dad, and did not talk down to me.

Mary F. Smith

That's just a sampling of typical Saturn customers comments, but can you guess the single word that I heard most often? *Friendly.* And notice how the Golden Rules are inherent in the comments. I took a look at the ingredients necessary to cook up those nice comments, and offer them to you as the following guidelines.

WHAT YOU CAN DO

In Person

For Managers:

- Hire for and train employees on "people skills." If they are meeting or talking to customers, they should know and practice basic common courtesy and communication skills.

For Everybody:

- Acknowledge every person when they enter your place of business. Don't ignore anyone because you feel that "it's not MY job" to greet customers. It is YOUR job! The job of everybody in the company is to serve customers, because customers are the reason you have a paycheck!

- Greet customers promptly. Have you ever been at the cashier's stand in a restaurant or store, with cash in hand ready to pay your bill or make your purchase, but nobody was around to take your money? (Does this mean it's free?)

- Smile—a genuine smile that lets people know you grasp the idea that they are your customers, and you're glad to see them. A smile can be contagious. When I visited a video store late one snowy afternoon, I was met by a smiling clerk, and in return, I smiled. He remarked that I was the first smiling customer he had all day. What a shame! Smiles put people at ease and make for a much more pleasant transaction.

- Use the customer's name if you know it. Wear your name tag if you have one.

- Dress professionally, in a manner that makes customers feel comfortable.

- Let each customer know that he or she is important to you, and that someone will be right there. Then make sure it happens!

- Treat your customers with respect, and don't "talk down" to them.

- View each customer in terms of a making him or her a long-time customer, and not in terms of a single transaction at the moment.

- Be honest and ethical.

- Don't let customers find you guilty of playing another version of "pass the customer." That's when customers see or talk to a real person, but have to go through a dozen other people before they get to the one that can help them. Is that the way you would want to be treated? If you're the first contact with a customer but can't answer his or her question, offer to find the answer or provide a solution. Pointing and giving directions to aisle 43 doesn't really help. Personally escort the customer if possible.

- Be aware of the messages that you send and receive through body language. One study looked at the impact between two or three people in an interpersonal communication scene, and investigated situations where people get "mixed" or inconsistent messages. All things being equal, when two people are in a situation, perhaps under stress (like buying a car), if the facial expression is not in sync with the spoken words, we tend to put more emphasis on the facial expression. The study found that a whopping 55 percent of the message is body language, 38 percent is tone of voice, and only 7 percent is content. You've probably experienced mixed messages when someone has said to you, "Have a nice day." The next time it happens, try to observe whether the other person's body language and tone of voice are consistent with the spoken message!

- Don't get carried away with interpreting body language. Just be a little bit conscious of yours AND that of your customer. For instance, proximity to the other person is also an element of body language. Some people are very uncomfortable with "in-your-face" closeness; many prefer a two-to three-foot comfort zone. Assuming that you didn't have garlic for lunch, if your customers keep backing away from you until they hit the wall, they're just "telling" you to back off. Give them the space they need.

- Be aware that there are several other elements of body language, including facial expression, the angle of your head, eye contact, posture, and gestures. Speaking of gestures, in a letter to Saturn, a 14-year-old girl (whose mother drives a Saturn) stated her belief that Saturn owners need a hand gesture. Something that says to other Saturn owners on the road, "Hey, nice car!" (No, Saturn—as a corporation—has not adopted a hand signal for owners. It feels this would be a fun thing for the owners to create or adopt on their own, or perhaps through local Saturn CarClubs. Any takers?)

With the Business Appearance

The showroom was very appealing and modern; clean and well-lighted. It had plenty of room and wasn't too confined.

Linda Umbenhen

The way you display your product or service, or convey your company image, is also very important in helping customers feel welcome. Saturn retail facilities are independently owned and maintained, but they are designed to certain standards. The design is all part of the process of making customers feel welcome by establishing a comfortable selling atmosphere. The *Detroit News* reported last year that Buick Division's new dealership designs would put it on a par with luxury line marketers like Lexus and Infiniti, *and* with Saturn.

Here are some customer impressions of Saturn retail facilities and their showrooms:

> *I really didn't notice anything special about the showroom. It didn't seem to be quite as cluttered as some other showrooms. I did see a display in one corner with Saturn hats and shirts. In fact, I later bought a shirt with Saturn on it. I'm proud of my Saturn, and I've never been proud of a car in my life.*
>
> Linda Bader

> *Clean, neat, functional, not overly "dressy."*
>
> Pat Garrity

> *It was new—in a trailer, with dirt roads. But inside, it was neat and clean.*
>
> Ed Champa

> *Comfortable, not intimidating.*
>
> Mary Lou Carver

> *I like that all Saturn retail facilities are the same—this indicates consistency and efficiency. They are modern, open, "clean" in style, smoke-free, and comfortable.*
>
> Lesia Bennett

> *The showroom was very clean and had a very open (welcoming) feeling.*
>
> Patti Clum

Bright, clean, open—the ladies' room is clean, cheery, and has "little touches" right down to soap and lotion from Bath & Body Works—how rare!

Lynn Holberton

Very clean, bright, and full of information.

Maureen Bunger

Everything was very organized.

Renee Minges

As you can see, once again we're talking about some pretty basic things, like clean, neat, bright, and organized. Saturn facilities are all those things, and more. Typically, showrooms include an accessible coffee and refreshments area, a display of "Saturn stuff" (shirts, caps, clothing, and things with the Saturn logo), literature display racks, and a touch-screen information system. But what I am getting at here are the important first few seconds when potential customers see a business—when they form an initial impression.

Customers don't tend to notice if the atmosphere or image matches their expectations. I was waiting in a client's store one day, on business, and was twice approached by shoppers looking for assistance. It seems that I had dressed the part, but their own employees had not. The lesson is that if something just doesn't match up, customers do take notice. Like the restaurant that's supposedly open at night, but the lights on the sign outside are turned off. Or the sign that's rusted and difficult to read. Or the real estate agent whose own house is the most dilapidated one on the block. And that's why Saturn facilities are neat and clean. That's why everyone is dressed appropriately, with many wearing Saturn-logo clothing. That's why the cars are shiny clean. That's why the Saturn name and logo are consistent in appearance. Your image is your business.

With the Business Appearance

Make sure you're not sending the UNWELCOME sign to customers. It's time to train those unbiased eyes on your business once again, and look at things from the prospective customer's viewpoint. When you're around the same place all the time, sometimes you just don't see things for what they really are. (Here's a good one for you: a lighting supply company's lamp-like sign—visible from the interstate—with burned-out lights!) Take a long, fresh, and observant look, both outside and inside, at:

- Signage and lighting
- Cleanliness and neatness of the premises, and ditto for company vehicles
- Reception or waiting areas
- Company uniforms or dress code
- Use of company name and logo

And don't just do this once a year. Add it to a monthly or weekly inspection checklist. Your list should identify the requirements for any given item; and provide space for the inspector's findings and for notes regarding any action that needs to be taken. For example, one item on your checklist might be the reception area. Requirements would include: adequate number of seats, comfortable chairs in good condition, and good lighting. If the inspector finds that five light bulbs need replacing and one chair needs repairs, the accompanying notes should identify who will take care of what, and when. Have a system to quickly handle these details, and make sure everything about your business does indeed say WELCOME.

The bottom line is this: helping customers to feel welcome smooths the path with an easy transition to the next step in the buying process—where they actually buy!

PRACTICE THE GOLDEN RULES

 KEY POINT

The entire Saturn experience invites the use of words like *family* and *friend,* even at this early welcoming stage of the buying process. Prospects who aren't even customers yet are exposed to this environment. This concept of treating prospects and customers like friends is foreign to many business people. I suppose the Golden Rules aren't typically thought of in business terms either. But just look at what Saturn has accomplished with this way of doing business.

I was once asked to write an article exploring the concept of, "Which comes first: the customer or the friend?" At that time (before I was exposed to the Saturn way of doing business), I concluded that there was no simple answer. After all, descriptive terms for the word *friend* in the dictionary range from acquaintance to mate, from supporter to confidant, and everything in between. Having said that, I'll let you draw your own conclusion. Just remember this: Creating new customers—or new friends—is all about building long-term relationships.

Help customers feel welcome by applying the Golden Rules to the way you treat people on the phone, in writing, in person, and with your business appearance. And don't expect customers to be proud of your business or product if you and your employees aren't also proud.

Make the Buying Process Easy

"I'm Ready to BUY!"

Saturn didn't act like they were selling the car to me, they let ME decide if I wanted to buy one or not. NO pressures and NO haggling.

Eric Penn

No Hassle, No Haggle

In a 10-year history of the J.D. Power and Associates New Car Sales Satisfaction Index Study, one principle has held true: Consumers do not like pressure during the sales process. Saturn recognized that from the start. That's why the company purposely set out to change this major part of the car-buying process, and dubbed it the "no-hassle, no-haggle" approach.

What made my buying experience pleasant? No pressure!! They were helpful but not pushy. I went back several times before deciding and not once was there any arm-twisting. All my ques-

tions were answered and then I was allowed to proceed at my own speed.

Lynn Holberton

No hassle means Saturn retailers are up-front about all elements of a vehicle's price. There are no last-minute add-ons or hidden charges. *No haggle* means the retailer sticks to a set price. There's no place for horse trading and dickering, because these don't fit with the Saturn philosophy. Saturn believes that no customer should ever wonder whether the retailer's next customer will get a better price by driving a harder bargain.

Personally, I always hated going shopping for a car. I didn't like playing the pricing game for hours. I didn't like the salesperson and the manager playing good guy/bad guy team tag. Then I discovered Saturn. Realizing that most people don't enjoy the negotiations and game-playing typically involved in buying a car, Saturn set out from the beginning to make things different. The company revolutionized the way cars are sold through its "no-hassle, no-haggle" approach. There is no pressure, no back-and-forth with the sales manager, no "must buy right now today!" demand. The price you see on the sticker is the price you pay. (Okay, so maybe some of you thrive on price-haggling. I've seen you in action at yard sales. For you, there will always be salespeople, somewhere, willing to accommodate your style.) So, Saturn blazed the trail by developing the perception that it's easy to do business with Saturn. Others have seen its success and tried to emulate it. One company's three-quarter-page ad in *USA Today* attempted to capture customers' attention with big and bold headlines shouting "NO HASSLE." But there's really more to the no-hassle, no-haggle approach as far as customers are concerned. And, this approach is important in creating the long-term relationship that leads to customer loyalty. Although price haggling may not be a factor in your business, there are plenty of lessons to be learned about this stage of the buying process.

According to a J.D. Power and Associates Special Report:

The cornerstone of Saturn's commitment to customer satisfaction is its sales approach, and one of the main reasons Saturn is highly effective in fulfilling its satisfaction commitment is the performance of its salespeople. Saturn topped the industry in the Salesperson Performance measure with a score of 159, which was 43 points higher than the industry average.

Salespeople at Saturn retail facilities are referred to as sales consultants. One woman from Indianapolis told me that she used to work for other dealerships, in the "old way" of selling and delivering cars. But now she's a Saturn sales consultant. "What a joy it is," she said, "to be working in a place where honesty is number one and customer enthusiasm is the driving force." To better understand this Saturn difference and why the salespeople are called consultants, take a look now at "The Saturn Consultative Sales Process." It was developed as a guide for sales consultants in assisting customers, and focuses on customers' wants and needs, in order to help them in the purchase decision-making process:

RECEPTION
All customers shall be greeted promptly and treated in a courteous, fair, and professional manner at all times.

INTERVIEWING
All customers shall receive a thorough interview in order for Sales Consultants to determine their wants and needs.

SELECTIVE WALKAROUND PRESENTATION
All customers shall receive a selective vehicle presentation based on their wants and needs.

DEMONSTRATION
All customers shall receive a complete vehicle demonstration ride, unless specifically declined.

PURCHASE CONSULTATION
All customers shall receive open and honest treatment about all elements of the transaction price.

DELIVERY
All customers shall receive a complete Saturn delivery of their new vehicle.

FOLLOW-UP
All customers shall be contacted at the following intervals after date of purchase: 3 days, 60 days, 5 months, annually.

We covered *Reception* in the last chapter. This chapter will cover *Interviewing, Selective Walkaround Presentation, Demonstration,* and *Purchase Consultation.* The next chapter (Chapter 8) covers *Delivery* and *Follow-Up.* Parts of these elements apply in almost every buying process, in every type of business. So, how does Saturn go about making the buying process easy?

It Starts with Training

I found out a couple of reasons why my salesman was so knowledgeable. He and his wife both owned Saturns, different models and years. He also told me about going to Spring Hill several times for training.

Lynn Smith

A New Car Sales Satisfaction Index Study by J.D. Power and Associates found that 71 percent of Saturn customers said their salesperson's knowledge of models and features was "excellent."

Making the buying process easy for customers begins with a knowledgeable, trained staff. *All the staff.* I've heard some employers reason that it's a waste of time to train employees, because many times they won't stay with the company long enough to make the training pay off. My answer to that is to quote Zig Ziglar:

> The only thing worse than training employees and losing them, is not training them and keeping them.

Saturn is a firm believer in training. Part of the Saturn Philosophy (Chapter 3) even states that:

We will develop the tools, training and education for each member, recognizing individual skill and knowledge.

In this section, we're dealing with training that is available to Saturn's retail team members, since they're the people customers deal with at this stage of the buying process. Notice that I used the word *available*. Retailers pay—per person—for most of the training. It's not fair to build a bunch of assumed training costs into the price of the car when different retailers have different training needs at different times, with different numbers of people to be trained. However, retailers are committed to the Saturn way, to growth and improvement, and to the importance of training. That's why they invest in training—anywhere from $155 per person for a four-hour course up to $1,025 per person for a three-day course. The costs vary depending partly on the type of course and location.

With *all the staff* in mind, Saturn developed a 1st Day Orientation course for new retail team members. The one-day course, presented at retail facilities, is designed to help team members understand the importance of their role within the retail team, and to introduce them to Saturn's unique customer focus, product, and culture. Upon completing the course, team members will be able to:

- Explain their individual role and responsibilities within the retail facility
- Understand their facility's guidelines and learn ways to support a safe and healthy environment
- Understand Saturn's mission, philosophy, values, and organizational culture
- Observe and begin to understand the Saturn Difference
- Learn about the Saturn vehicle and receive a first-hand driving experience

Since the course is formatted as a guided learning experience, it can be facilitated by one or more of the retailer's team members. Every step of the content is outlined in an easy-to-follow Leader Guide. It's also flexible enough so that retail-specific information can be incorporated. Lectures and discussions are combined with the opportunity for individuals to analyze how they personally contribute to creating customer enthusiasm by developing a personal action plan. Information that team members learn about the product (cars) is reinforced with a demonstration drive.

For retail team members who have contact with customers, there's also the Customer Contact Skills course (described in Chapter 6).

As part of initial training, there's also a day-and-a-half Spring Hill Orientation course. Here's the opportunity for retail team members to visit Spring Hill and experience Saturn firsthand. It includes a plant tour, a ride-and-drive to learn more about the car, and team building events at the Excel course. Here's what participants are expected to be able to do upon completing the course:

- Explain Saturn's mission and philosophy, and their significance to Saturn team members
- Experience and apply Saturn values

- Describe UAW and other Saturn partnerships
- Describe Saturn history highlights
- Explain the concept of Customer Enthusiasm
- Describe a "Moment of Truth" and its impact on Customer Enthusiasm
- Describe unique product features

Now it's on to more training. A real must for beginning sales consultants is the three-and-one-half-day Consultative Sales Workshop, which can logically follow the Spring Hill Orientation course (above). This is the class that teaches how to utilize the Saturn consultative sales process to achieve customer enthusiasm. One thing that participants will learn is that flexibility is built into the process, to ensure that the experience is always customer-driven. The workshop format allows people to learn and practice the concepts, and is built on participant input and group activities. Here's what participants should be able to do upon completing this course:

- Use the Saturn Consultative Sales Process to demonstrate the Saturn Difference to customers
- Conduct objective competitive comparisons for guests
- Demonstrate product knowledge and presentation skills
- Explain the Saturn Financial Services Consultation Process, the Saturn Used Car Process and Saturn Brand Critical Standards

After looking at that list, does it occur to you also that there's some cross-training going on? I'm for it. When I purchased my car, my sales consultant was indeed knowledgeable about financial services, even though he wasn't the one to handle that process. It's one more way that the buying process is made easy.

Remember Saturn's value of "continuous improvement"? Well, ongoing training is a part of it. There's a four-hour continuous learning Sales Refresher Seminar offered on a regional basis. It includes a review of the consultative sales process with attention focused on what is changing, reemphasizing customer enthusiasm, and reinforcing the sales consultant's ability to address customer concerns. Recently added for discussion were results of a study sharing what customers are saying: that they want to be empowered when making a purchasing decision. The intent of the refresher seminar is to have the participants leave with renewed enthusiasm for the Saturn process.

The training for retailers doesn't stop yet. There's a one-day course on Retail Employee Selection Tools, designed for managers who are involved in the hiring process. For sales consultants in particular, it's critical to select a person who not only is a good match for the position, but who also fits the Saturn culture. Several retail managers told me that they tend not to hire experienced car salespeople from the industry, since Saturn's way of doing business is different from the usual car-selling environment. Many of the employees at Saturn's retail facilities are also so knowledgeable because they *own* a Saturn. They speak from personal experience, since lots of them were Saturn customers *before* they were ever employed by a Saturn retailer. Seems that their exposure to the Saturn culture made a lasting impression, and one that they wanted to be part of. That's how it was at Saturn of Louisville for a customer turned sales consultant. She explained, "I've been a Saturn owner for four-and-a-half years now. Right away, I fell in love with the car and the dealership." At one retail store that I visited in Kentucky, 8 out of 15 sales consultants were customers before they became employees. Some become customers after they become employees. That was the case with my sales consultant. Not long after the first Saturns hit the road, and before he knew anything about them, he witnessed a serious accident. A new Saturn got thoroughly smashed, but the two women in it emerged apparently unhurt. A year or two later, he noticed a help-wanted ad in the paper inviting people to "sell something from out of this world." Those interested in applying were invited to bring their spouses along for the initial interview. (Remember—it's a relationship-building, family thing.) Then he recalled the accident involving the Saturn. Well, he got the job, and today he and his wife both own Saturns.

The education process also happens at retail product meetings and annual business conferences. Some of the hard-to-believe enthusiastic customer stories come to life at the conferences as Saturn brings real customers in to share their stories with the retailers. It helps remind them what customer enthusiasm is all about. The retailers love it, and leave revitalized.

Retailers continuously conduct their own in-house training also. Saturn of Louisville, for example, holds a half-hour coaching session each morning for service and sales consultants. Team members help train each other, and individuals share their perspective on a particular topic. In addition, there are one-hour meetings on Saturday and Monday mornings for all team members.

That's not all, folks. Supplemental and advanced training is available on topics like leadership, retail team building, follow-up and networking, and used-car process sales training. You'll read more about some of these—plus others—in subsequent chapters. Oh, yeah, I should also note that Saturn makes the training accessible by presenting it in a variety of places—on-site and off-site, at Spring Hill, at retail facilities, and at hotel conference rooms. And that trainers include a variety of people—team members that contribute in their area of expertise, Saturn's regular training team, and outside professionals.

The long and short of it is that training is part of the foundation on which customer loyalty builds. Enthusiastic employees help make for enthusiastic customers. It's difficult to have one without the other. Can you teach enthusiasm? Only if your mission statement, values, and the way you do business continually reinforce it. It has to be genuine. And, it will help if you make training part of a continuous improvement value.

WHAT YOU CAN DO

Training

- Provide initial training—about the company, products, services, and how customers use and benefit from your products and services.
- Provide ongoing training.
- Provide extra "people skills training" to all customer contact people.
- Continue to train.
- Use a variety of trainers—in-house trainers, outside speakers, and suppliers or distributors. Use authorities in your field and those outside your field with a different perspective. Use customer success (and failure stories) to train. Have coworkers teach each other and share "best practices."
- Keep training.
- Train in different settings—on-site and off-site. Field trips. A combination of seminars, staff meetings, lunch-and-learn programs, college courses, continuing education classes, or interactive distance learning.
- Cross-train people on other jobs, either formally or just to create awareness. Have technicians spend a day with salespeople, visiting customers. Put office people in the field for a day.
- Provide different ways to learn. Mix up the serious with the fun. Include role-playing exercises, quizzes, and team exercises. Use audio, video, books, slides, computerized training

modules, overheads, flip charts, post-it papers on the wall, or play with games and toys.

- Train some more. (You're beginning to get the idea. Remember: *continuous improvement.*)

Don't skip over this part if you're a one-person business or the company owner. You need training too, although you may choose to call it "professional development." Operating a business takes many different skills, and it's difficult to be proficient in every topic. Keep yourself current in your particular field or industry, and seek training in your areas of weakness, whether they're sales, computers, or accounting. Look for learning opportunities provided by manufacturers whose products you represent. And learn from mentors or others in your industry who have been there, done that, or are going through it now. Team up with an indirect competitor in another town and learn from each other. I know of an office furniture and supply company whose owners meet several times a year with owners from similar companies in surrounding states. (The name of the group: I.M.O.K.—representing the companies' home states of Indiana, Michigan, Ohio, and Kentucky.) They don't compete directly in the same territories, so the arrangement gives them an opportunity to both help and learn from each other.

Providing Information

I made the decisions with the information all in front of me.
William M. Machuga

The prices were up front. I knew what I'd be paying as I added on extras.
Kim E. Cox

Okay, so everybody at the retail facility is now trained and knowledgeable. But what about the customers? Providing easy-to-understand information helps make the buying process easy—and helps educate customers. When Saturn arrived on the scene, people did not know what to expect. Customers weren't used to buying cars in a no-haggle manner. Expectations on how they would be treated were low. Saturn has had to educate customers and make it easy for folks to understand. Saturn is great at this in so many ways—in addition to all that information that's in the sales consultants' heads.

There are several easy ways for people to get Saturn information before they ever set foot in a showroom. Calling the toll-free number for potential buyer inquiries (described in Chapter 6) is one way. Saturn's web site on the Internet (briefly described in Chapter 5) is another way. One potential customer shopping for cars requested information from several car companies' web sites. She later sent an e-mail to Saturn, saying that she had been impressed by its being the only company to send a pricing sheet along with the catalog, and had wondered what everyone else was trying to hide. She cited this as another example of how much Saturn does to make car buying easy, and thanked the company for making her first car-buying experience such a good one. (Yes, of course she ended up buying a Saturn.) Saturn has received various e-mail messages from customers indicating that the information provided via the web site or e-mail led them to buy.

Information available on Saturn's web site that would help people at this stage of the buying process includes, for each model: colors and fabrics, features, pricing, and specs. And then there's the Interactive Pricing Center where you can do lots of useful things, like calculate monthly payments or begin the credit application process. Other information on the web site lets you order a brochure, find the nearest retailer, and bone up on the used-cars inspection process.

Saturn makes it easy for people to get information. Displays in retail showrooms include a touch-screen computer system for visitors' use that covers all sorts of information about Saturn Corporation, the cars, the manufacturing process, and so on. Audio and video combine to present the information in an easy-to-understand manner.

Saturn gladly makes available detailed price lists with options, plus booklets excerpted from IntelliChoice's *The Complete Car Cost Guide* (see Exhibit 7.1). These booklets contain a model-by-model account of purchase price, ownership costs (projected), warranty/maintenance information, resale value, cumulative costs, and ratings on "ownership cost value." (Six ratings range from poor to excellent; all 1998 Saturn models are rated as excellent.)

Saturn makes it easy from every angle. Stop by a retail facility and pick up any Saturn brochure or literature. Take a look, and you'll find that it is simply written in conversational-style language like the example from a brochure on used cars (see Exhibit 7.2). (Even the *Owner's Handbook* is actually understandable and usable. How many of you can say that about your car manual?) Their complete product catalog is interesting and fun to read, in addition to being informational. The cover of the 36-page 1998 catalog doesn't even show a car. In black and white, it shows the back of a little boy—in midair—jumping off a dock into a lake. The headline, in small letters, is "A Moment In Time." Inside, in addition to photos and information about the cars, there's a lot of neat stuff. Like stories and photos that we can relate to, that make it easier for us to understand. Information on the jobs of team members, about team building, about the manufacturing process, about the retailers and Saturn in the community, and even a few real customer stories. In the back you'll find everything you ever wanted to know about features and options, specifications, and other vital information.

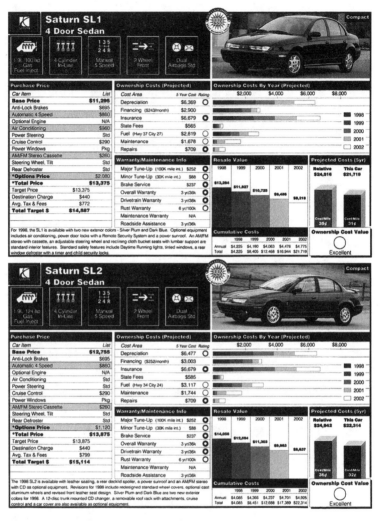

Exhibit 7.1   Excerpt from IntelliChoice *The Complete Car Cost Guide*

Saturn also makes it easy to understand about risks and guarantees. The owner protection plan brochure clearly and simply states the Saturn money-back guarantee:

> In a nutshell, the policy is that you can return a vehicle if you're not completely satisfied—just so long as it's within the first 30

As Saturn retailers, we seem to have made some waves with the different way we sell cars. People are genuinely surprised when they don't get pounced upon the moment they walk in our door. Or when they don't have to wrestle with anyone to get a fair price. Some people even find themselves grinning. In the middle of a car showroom. Imagine that.

Now imagine selling used cars in the exact same way. For us, it wasn't much of a stretch. After all, we had the store, we had the people and we had the philosophy—the basic belief being that, when it comes down to it, nobody wants you to "sell" them a car. What they really want is for you to help them buy one. And if you check a used car out, back it up with all sorts of unexpected stuff, including a bunch of committed people, and sell it right alongside your new cars, you're bound to make customers pretty happy.

And that, rather neatly, brings us back to the notion of grinning in a car showroom. Which may not seem so preposterous, after all. But then, maybe that's just us. (Actually, if you shop around, it seems it is just us.)

"When it came to buying a used car, they didn't make us feel like second-class citizens."
—The McCandless Family

Exhibit 7.2 Page from Saturn Used Car Brochure

days or 1,500 miles of ownership, whichever comes first. You can either select another Saturn or get a full refund of the purchase price.

Okay, so there are a few details, but they're reasonable and understandable; not lots of complicated fine-print. One of Saturn's retailer owners expressed her opinion that Saturn's guarantee helps make it easy for customers to buy:

> We so liked the concept that we carried it over into all of our non-Saturn dealerships. We think it's a customer-friendly way to do business. People say, "How can you do that?" We say, "How can we afford NOT to do that?" Say a person loses their job or has a health problem or illness and needs to return that vehicle. Some day they'll be in the market for a car again, and they'll think good things about us, and we hope they'll come back to us.

Even Saturn's *used* cars come with a 3-day money-back guarantee, and the same 30-day/1,500-mile trade-in policy. It's all explained in an 8-page pocket-size brochure with a cover that states "When you buy a used car from a Saturn retailer, you can only depend on a couple of things." Inside, you'll find those couple things explained. Okay, I know that cover statement got your interest, so I'll let you in on those couple things:

> Number One: More than you're used to. (More quality, more security, more choice.)
>
> Number Two: Less than you're used to. (No haggle, no hassle, no fear.)

The brochure then goes on to explain why "what you see is what you get." It explains that cars with red labels are certified used Saturns, and what's involved in the inspection. Among other things, a red label means that the car is less than five model years old, with under 60,000 miles. Another section lists what you get after you buy. And finally, the brochure describes similar information on cars with green labels—other used Saturns and other makes of used cars. According to another brochure, Saturn puts every qualified used car they sell through a 150-point-plus inspection and reconditioning process that "sniffs out everything from a dysfunctional EGR valve to an old cracker crumb lurking in the glove compartment." This process and the color-coded window labels make used-car buying easy for the customer, eliminating worry and offering peace of mind. So even if the customers buy non-Saturn used cars, they still get treated in the treat-people-right Saturn way.

As you can see, Saturn provides information for potential buyers in various ways—by phone via the toll-free number, by mail, through the web site, and easy-to-understand printed materials. Potential customers can obtain and peruse the information at their convenience. And all of that helps make it easier for them to buy.

WHAT YOU CAN DO

Providing Information

Make it easy for your prospective customers to understand about your company, products, services, pricing, and the way business is done.

- Ask other people not familiar with your business to look over your brochures and printed literature. Get an unbiased perspective on whether the information presented is easy to understand. This also applies to users' manuals, guides, or instructions.

- Make a list of the ways someone could obtain information about your products and services. Are these ways easy for prospective customers to access? Are they readily available when and where your prospective customers would likely seek them?

- Promote access to information. If you have a toll-free phone number, advertise it! Print it on business cards, brochures, mailing labels, and packages. The same goes for e-mail and web site addresses. Otherwise, how are people going to know how to find information on your business?

- Make a list of the types or kinds of information available. Could answers to 90 percent of your prospective customers' questions be answered by that available information? Is everything there, and up-to-date? Make sure that the information is not vague, or that one brochure doesn't contradict the information in another one.

- Take a fresh look at your warranty and guarantee information. You don't have to put your lawyer out of a job, but get rid of the fine print and legalese. If you're using a warranty or guarantee as a marketing tool to attract customers (which is a very good idea), come up with something that makes it attractive and easy to understand (for customers that is, not lawyers). I heard about one couple shopping for plants in a new garden center. When they asked an employee about any kind of guarantee if the plants didn't survive, they were told yes, the guarantee was on the back of the purchase receipt. Only when they got home did they read the receipt, which stated, "We guarantee our plants to grow—or die trying." Well, at least it's easy to understand!

Discovering Customer Wants and Needs

I bought a Saturn, but at first I was really interested in a car at a different dealership. I asked the salesman there about anti-lock brakes. He replied, "It's very technical, you wouldn't understand." Well, it so happens that I have a degree in mechanical

*electronics, and told the salesman that I thought I could handle
it. He lost the sale, but not because of the car. At Saturn, my
experience was totally different.*

Stephen Murgan

Now we get into the meat of what Saturn refers to as the "consultative sales process." But you won't get very far if you don't
first understand how customers want to be treated. Looks like
the Golden Rules come into play once again. Making the buying
process easy doesn't mean "dumbing it down" or assuming that
your customers are stupid. Customers want to be treated as
intelligent people. And they want to know that they are making
intelligent buying decisions. Remember, "Trust and respect for
the individual" is one of Saturn's five values.

So what exactly does a "consultative sales process" mean?
Consider the meaning of the word *consult,* and you'll get the
idea. Definitions include "to seek advice or information; to take
into account, consider; to keep in mind while acting or deciding; to show regard for." To me, it means considering the sales
process as more than just a one-time sale. It means the beginning of building long-term relationships with customers, so
they'll keep coming back. It requires working with each customer to determine that individual's wants and needs. It
requires applying the following four of Saturn's "Six Steps to
Customer Enthusiasm" (all six steps appear in Chapter 4):

1. LISTEN to your Customers . . . don't assume; ask . . . seek
   to understand their specific needs, desires and expectations.

2. Create an environment of MUTUAL TRUST . . . be caring and responsive to Customer requests. Be honest and
   timely, do not build false expectations.

3. Think in terms of EXCEEDING CUSTOMER EXPEC-
   TATIONS. Do what is right for the Customer . . . stand

behind Saturn products and services. Strive to go the extra step that transforms Customer satisfaction into CUSTOMER ENTHUSIASM.

4. MAKE IT HAPPEN . . . SPEED is essential . . . Create a "WIN-WIN" culture and environment for the Customer, the dealer, and Saturn.

The capitalization and bolding of certain words is Saturn's choice, with which I wholeheartedly agree. Take SPEED for instance. We live in an "instant" world, and time is precious. Expectations of "timely" are high. Everybody wants everything yesterday. Your time is valuable, and so is that of your customer. Being timely, caring, responsive, and honest while discovering a customer's wants and needs requires one more thing. It's the first word in Step 1: Listen. A Greek philosopher named Epictetus is credited with the quote, "Nature has given to men one tongue, but two ears, that we may hear from others twice as much as we speak."

So, by listening to your customers, you learn. Granted, sometimes listening is just not easy to do. We really have to condition ourselves to work at it, and learn to listen. We're all guilty of hearing but not really listening (you know, like with your spouse, or when a parent is trying to tell you something). I have tuned in the radio many times to hear the weather forecast. Before I know it, the weather forecast is over and a song has started, but I don't have a clue about the temperature or predictions. I heard, but I didn't listen.

Now, let the Saturn interviewing process begin. A sales consultant named Eddie, after a prompt and courteous greeting, listened as I described my situation and what I thought I wanted in a car. He asked lots of questions, and we conversed as he tried to figure out what was important to me. Whenever Eddie discovered a key piece of information, he'd jot it down in a small pocket notebook. We looked over a few cars on the lot as he helped me discover the differences between the various models. Then we moved into the showroom where the interviewing process continued, and I got to see the cutaway car. He described some of the highlights, and let me try to put a dent into the polymer car door—only to watch it pop right back out. Then it was back out to the lot, where we located a car that met most of my wants and needs. I was treated to the "selective walkaround presentation," where Eddie described and I experimented with the various features of the car. This was a learning experience for me, with lots of neat little discoveries along the way. Don't need the car ashtray? Just pop it out and in it's place you have an extra cup holder. Driver's seat doesn't fit your back contour just right? Use the lumbar adjustment.

By that time, I was thoroughly impressed and informed, and Eddie already knew more about my wants and needs than the last six salespeople combined at other car dealerships. And I was very much at ease. Is this sounding different to you? Different than your last car-buying experience? You be the judge.

On to the test drive, or what Saturn refers to as the demonstration ride. There were some slight differences between this test drive and ones from my past experiences. The walkaround presentation I'd just received was so thorough that I was able to make all the adjustments (or they were made for me) before I started driving, which is a heck of a lot safer than during the drive. You know, things like the seat adjustment, shoulder restraint strap height, radio, and heat/air conditioning controls. And during the drive, the interview continued. Most of my questions were anticipated; some were even answered before I could I ask them. Eddie continued to consult and take notes.

After the demonstration, it was back to the showroom. We were comfortably seated in an open office area. (Nothing to hide, no "secret" negotiations!) Let me back up for a moment and explain the "we." My husband accompanied me on this visit, but we made it clear at the start that this was going to be my car and my decision. Eddie treated us just right, involving my husband only as he wanted to be involved, but directing his focus on me. I have been in buying situations before where I would ask a question, but the salesperson would address the answer to my husband, as if I didn't exist.

Eddie offered to get us some soft drinks, and during the short time he was gone, every single Saturn person that passed greeted us with a smile and asked if we were being helped. When Eddie returned, the discussion continued. I used the word *discussion* intentionally, because that's exactly what it was. Eddie made the process easy at this point, since he had already determined my wants and needs. That's where his notebook came in handy, as he began preparing my vehicle want-list. He knew what options might interest me, and presented them in a way that I could understand and decide if they would indeed be beneficial. For example, because of the interviewing process, he knew that I did some traveling in my business, so he suggested the cruise control option. He explained which extras really were standard on the model I was considering, which gave me reassurances that I would be getting value for my money. There was a smooth transition to the "purchase consultation" part of the process. The whole time, Eddie was handling everything for me himself, without having to run to a sales manager. Of course, all the prices were right there in front of me, and I knew that I would not have to play the price negotiation game. I could see the bottom line as I added or subtracted options. There was never any pressure. And based on what friends had told me, I knew that if I had decided just to leave and "think it over," that would be okay with Eddie. There would be no arm-twisting.

But then, Eddie sensed my hesitation. The car that I test drove and that met all my other wants and needs—well, I had just decided that the interior wasn't the right color. Eddie understood. He double-checked every car on the lot for the right combination of colors and options—with no luck. And no prospect of ordering it, since it was the end of the model year. Not to panic, though, or to settle for less. In a matter of about five minutes, Eddie returned with good news. He had located the car I wanted, with the right colors and options. The bad news was that I couldn't have it that day. See, it was located at another Saturn retail facility–in Ohio, and 160 miles away. Yes, I wanted it. Would it cost extra? Nope. We left then, with assurances that they would get the car and call me. Sure enough, the next morning, I received a call from Eddie, explaining that he would be driving to Ohio later in the day to get the car. Eddie called again that evening to tell me that my car was now in Louisville, safe and sound. When would I like to come in and get it?

Only later, when I asked, did I discover what took place behind the scenes. First, it meant a quick search of a database to locate the car at another retail facility—a process made easy since Saturn facilities are connected by satellite to a great computer system. Then, the two retailers had to agree on an equitable car swap and process all the paperwork. Eddie then drove there and back—on his own time. The retailer had anticipated that these swaps would be needed from time to time to meet customer needs, and had budgeted money to cover expenses. But what it took to accomplish all of this was invisible to me— as some actions should be to your customers. They don't really want or need to know how much trouble you have to go through, or what's involved with your system.

WHAT YOU CAN DO

Discovering Customer Wants and Needs

Think how turned off you were by the last canned sales presentation that was thrust at you—before you ever had a chance to say a word. You didn't buy, did you? Customers need someone to listen to their wants, decipher their needs, and act as a consultant for and with them (just like a best friend would). What you can do in this part of the process is apply the first four steps of Saturn's "Six Steps to Customer Enthusiasm" (listed at the beginning of this section), which serve as a basis for these tips:

- *Start with the right attitude.* Enter this stage of the buying/selling process with a win/win attitude. In a win/lose situation, there is no real winner. One of Saturn's steps refers to "mutual trust," which is only possible with a win/win environment. And the step that calls for "trust and respect for the individual" doesn't work if you assume that customers are stupid.

- *Listen.* Do it right by:

   Concentrating

   Listening optimistically and keeping your mind open

   Holding your emotions in check and not jumping to conclusions

   Listening for ideas—not just facts

   Listening in the present and not be thinking about what you're going to say

- *Lead the way.* As much as possible, have one person handle the process from beginning to end. If the expertise or help of others is needed, you should seek out that other person, not make the customer do it. Don't just tell customers where or how to find something—lead the way and show them. When I visited a particular music store, a young gentlemen (kid, to me) greeted me at the door, and politely asked if he could assist me. After I told him what I was looking for, I almost went into shock when he not only escorted me to the section and showed me the available selections, but actually spoke knowledgeably about my options! And this has happened every time I've visited that store! At a competitor's store, when the only clerk present finally hung up the phone from her personal conversation, she merely pointed in the general direction towards the section of my interest. Need I say that I didn't buy at that store?

- *Wisely present options.* At this stage of the buying process, you should know your potential customer well enough to present "customized options"—those choices that you believe would appeal to or apply to that particular customer. Say you have 10,001 options available for the customer. Color, style, type, size, accessories, new versus used, and on and on. Lay the whole shebang on the table and you will overwhelm the customer. Most of us like to have choices, but only to a certain extent. Years ago, when we were having a house built, I discovered just how many hundreds of choices there were and an equal number of decisions to be made. My breaking point came when the builder called for the umpteenth time that week and asked what color grout I wanted for the entrance foyer floor tiles. Aaaggghhh! Please, no more decisions! Many choices can and should be anticipated and addressed early in the buying process—by the salesperson, not the customer. Your task at this point is to ask yourself, "What will be of most benefit to the customer?" Also, the choices should be presented more knowledgeably. Instead of: "We have 12 standard colors and 500 custom colors," it could be: "You have chosen blue tiles and we recommend this particular shade of gray to match. Do you agree, or would you care to see other colors?"

- *Review internal policies, procedures, and systems.* Do these elements of your business benefit the customer? Are they truly necessary? Or do they exist merely because "this is the way it's always been done." Could they be done differently? Don't waste your customers' time and money because of complicated or unnecessary internal processes. Once during a compliance audit at a hospital, the auditor found that when employees in one department were utilizing certain supplies, they would meticulously record usage details like exact amount, date, name, etc. Everybody knew that they were supposed to do it, but nobody knew why. It turned out that several years earlier someone (long since gone) had misinterpreted a regulation. So for years, the employees never knew that all that extra recording was really not necessary. What a waste of employees' time, the extra time that it took to serve patients (i.e., customers), and money!

- *Fill out forms for customers.* Don't make them continue to repeat the same information again and again. My sales consultant took down the relevant information once, then completed every part of the forms he possibly could. When I take my car in for service, the service advisor simply enters my vehicle identification number in the computer, and—BAM!—instantly has my name, address, and so forth. I don't have to fill out the form or repeat information that they already have. When I place orders over the phone with companies that I've already done business with—like the pizza delivery company—it's nice that they have my address and I don't have to repeat it.

- *Under-promise and over-deliver.* Don't build false expectations, and your customers might be as overjoyed as these Saturn customers:

> *We couldn't find a car on the lot with all the options that we wanted, so we ordered one. Our sales consultant would call every day and keep us updated. One day, he said "It's on the line." Then soon, "It's on the truck." [About a day after it was loaded on the truck] he called and said, "Guess what? Your car is here!" It didn't take nearly as long as we thought it might. We were overjoyed!*
>
> Charles A. and Lou Chamberlain

- *Go the extra mile.* Make it as easy as possible for the customer, just like one Saturn retailer did for Brad:

After my Toyota had been in the repair shop for ten days and still wasn't finished, I went to a Saturn dealership. I couldn't believe that they actually sent an appraiser over to the Toyota shop, in order to make me an offer for my trade-in. They helped me find exactly what I wanted, made it easy, and put the whole deal together. And I was only purchasing a used Saturn!"

Brad Houts

Show Me the Money!

I thought that might get your attention! Now for the getting-paid part. Sure, some credit card companies brag that certain establishments only accept THEIR card and not others. If you're a customer with the OTHER credit card, well, they're not making it easy for you, are they? Saturn's financing tools aren't any different from what most major car dealers have. It's how Saturn presents the payment options and treats customers during this process that makes the difference. Surprised?

The finance or payment process at Saturn is part of the consultative sales process. The whole system is designed to keep customers coming back. The finance team member goes through the same process of listening and presenting the right options that meet the needs of each customer. As for the mass of paperwork that is required for financing, each form is first explained to the customer. You're not left to figure out the fine print on your own, nor are you asked to "just sign it." Even before new laws were enacted requiring full disclosure on leases, Saturn was ahead of the game. Their set, no-haggle pricing and disclosure forms made it easy for customers to understand what they were getting. Saturn's money-back guarantee is further reassurance that puts some customers at ease during this process. Plus, there are no unpleasant "surprise" add-ons at this point.

One option offered to me—as part of the finance process—is another way that Saturn makes it easy for customers to continue to do business with them after the purchase. It's a service plan called Saturn Car Care. It was offered after the finance person discovered (during the interview process) that neither my husband nor I care to change the oil or do regular maintenance on the car ourselves. But I do care about taking care of my Saturn, and I prefer that the folks who are best qualified are the ones who do the work. The Car Care plan was my answer. It includes all the regularly scheduled maintenance recommended by Saturn, like oil changes, filter replacements, lubrication, tire rotation, new spark plugs, and brake inspections. For a price less than what I would normally pay for all of these things separately over the years, I painlessly financed the cost of coverage. That's a one-time, up-front payment and I know exactly what I'm paying for. There are four different plan options based on the desired years/miles of coverage. Now, whenever I take my car in for routine service, we both know exactly which services will be done. And here's the best part: It's already paid for! Well, at least by the bank. I don't have to pay any money out of my pocket at the time of service. I consider it a real convenience, and that much more value for my money.

WHAT YOU CAN DO

Show Me the Money!
(Payment and Financing Options)

- DO NOT make the mistake of basing your payment or finance terms solely on whatever makes it easy for your accounting department. Folks in the accounting department work FOR the customer (as does everybody else).

- DO give customers options, and make it easy for them to pay for your products and services (that is, assuming you DO want your money!). Build some flexibility into your policies and procedures. Be reasonable. (Three months in a row, I received in the mail an invoice from a long-distance phone service company for one cent. How much reason went into that?!)

- DO make sure that your people responsible for handling money transactions for customers are aware of the payment options that are available. If you're that person, take the time to learn the options. (Isn't it amazing when a server who brings the check to your table at the restaurant doesn't know which credit cards are acceptable?)

- DO look for ways to build in value for your customers through the payment or finance process. Remember, it's not just a one-time transaction. Even if everything else has gone smoothly up to this point, a misstep here could mean the loss of the customer for both this sale and future ones.

GO THE EXTRA MILE

KEY POINT

A couple in New York wanted to surprise their daughter with a new Saturn as a graduation gift, but knew she would not be returning home from school in California over the summer. They visited a Saturn dealer in New York—who promptly handled everything. The car was ordered and purchased, registered in New York, then shipped to a retailer in California. The California dealer then took over by helping set up the surprise, decorating the car, and joining in the celebration as it was presented to the couple's daughter.

(Continues)

(Continued)

Then there's the true story, told in a Saturn commercial, about a woman living in a small town that doesn't even have a stoplight, much less a car dealership. So when she wanted to look at a Saturn, she called the closest retailer, even though it was "all the way down in Salt Lake." No problem, they said, we'll pick you up. See, the sales guy was also a pilot. And 250 miles later, she bought the gold one, and remarked, "Good thing, I guess, considering that no one had ever mentioned how I was gonna get home."

You DO need to go the extra mile to make it easy for customers to buy from you, though perhaps 250 miles is extreme. Your trip through the process can start as early as creating a positive perception about purchasing, long before a customer ever visits your place of business, or picks up the phone to order. Remember, those loyal, enthusiastic customers do talk.

Make the buying process easy for customers through preparation—by learning and listening, and using a consultative approach to discover their wants and needs. Make it easy for customers and prospects to get information—how, where, and when they want it. Make the information easy to understand. Simplify and modify internal processes, with the customer in mind. Proceed at the customer's pace, and don't hassle. Present options in a customized manner. Have flexible payment policies that makes sense for your customers, and that reinforce value.

> *Saturn has definitely taken the right approach to selling cars. It's about time that a company has learned that customers are people, too. I like to leave a dealership feeling like I was treated fairly and courteously.*
>
> John Sillavan

Communicate AFTER
The Sale

"Don't Forget Me Now!"

Saturn still makes us feel like part of the family by sending newsletters, Christmas cards, and an anniversary card on our purchase date. These "little things" are great!

Linda and David Umbenhen

Communication AFTER the sale is where Saturn really shines. And this is where you can really wax right on by your competition. Because, unfortunately, this is the point where too many businesses stall, sputter, and die. (Which, fortunately for you, makes this step a wide-open area for improvement!)

Technically, when does "after the sale" begin? That will depend on your business. Given that this whole process of creating customer loyalty is continuous, let's start early with the "delivery" part of the process.

Delivery

When I went to pick up my car, it was a ROYAL event! Just like my 50th birthday party all over again. They took my picture, gave me the Saturn cheer, and everybody was clapping as I drove away. It makes you feel like you just really accomplished something big.

Linda Bader

Saturn begins communicating immediately, with "delivery" of the car that makes customers feel special and appreciated. Saturn doesn't dictate delivery details to their retailers, other than to say, "Celebrate it!" So, each retailer does something a little different, but the following description is fairly typical. You may have even seen it on a Saturn commercial, but didn't believe it was for real. Trust me—I lived through one and witnessed others—it is for real.

If the customer hasn't already been given a tour of the facility and service area, that is done. He or she is introduced to the service manager and told about hours of operation and phone numbers. After all the buying and payment details have been worked out, a salesperson gives their customer a thorough introduction to the Saturn owner's manual. Guarantees, warranties, and roadside assistance programs are reviewed. Then, it's on to the car.

This is where the fun begins. THE CAR now occupies a prime show-off spot (sometimes referred to as the "launch pad") in the showroom. Next to it is a sign, proclaiming to all, something along the lines of: "A NEW SATURN SL2 FOR VICKI." The car is sparkling clean, with not a speck of dirt or smudge. The customer is then introduced again to the various features of the car, including two real must-dos: how to set the clock and how to operate the radio. The seat and mirrors are adjusted to suit the driver. On the dashboard, next to all the candy or flowers, is a card congratulating the customer on the purchase and thanking him or her for choosing a Saturn. It's from the Saturn Team, "wishing you the best" and hoping "that you feel every bit as good about driving it, as we do building it."

The customer is welcome to take another test drive, just to make sure everything is as it should be.

Now the customer thinks that he or she is ready to drive away. But first, a photo is taken of the happy owner standing next to the new Saturn. Then, an announcement goes out, and all available Saturn team members gather around the customer and their new car. The salesperson introduces the customer and says a few words about the purchase. Then comes the Saturn cheer . . . clap to a beat . . . and chant . . . on a count of three . . . "I SAY, YOU SAY, WE SAY, SATURN!" Members of the team come forward to shake hands with the customer, offer congratulations and a reminder that they are all a team and that anyone, anytime is willing to help. And the happy customer drives out of the showroom in the shiny new car, with a big smile.

Only Saturn customers would understand why my sales consultant's license plate reads "I SAY."

Delivery of products or services can take place in different ways. My Saturn CarClub membership kit was UPS-delivered to my home in a plain white corrugated cardboard box. It was the label that caught my attention. It covered most of the box's top surface, and half of it had a bright yellow and red striped border, resembling a caution tape. Inside the border, in big letters, it read: "Caution: Contents of this box may cause intense enthusiasm, fanatic behavior and excessive amounts of fun." Makes you want to tear it open on the spot!

Saturn checks itself on a different means of "delivery"— when I deliver my car to them for service. My service consultant initiates a "Customer Service Interaction Checklist" (see Exhibit 8.1) for both his signature and mine. It serves as a "Yes or Not Applicable" reminder of six areas that should be offered to me at the time of delivery. It reminds them to offer me the services, and it reinforces value and communication with me.

Customer Service Interaction Checklist

SATURN. OF LOUISVILLE   SATURN SERVICE 502-499-3800

YES	N/A		
☐	☐	1. Received Written Estimate of Cost	$
☐	☐	2. Received Written Time Promise for Completion TIME	
☐	☐	3. Extended an Offer of a Free Car Wash	
☐	☐	4. Recommended Any Additional Services That Are Needed	
☐	☐	5. Offered a Road Test With Technician to Verify Complaint	
☐	☐	6. Customer Address Current with Service Order	NEW ADDRESS

X _____   X _____
    Customer's Signature   Service Consultant's Signature

Exhibit 8.1   Customer Service Interaction Checklist

WHAT YOU CAN DO

Delivery

- If there is some time lag between actual purchase and delivery, you have an even greater opportunity to impress customers—and further communicate—with the delivery of your product or service. Do you have a local industrial customer that is really hurting for delivery of that process part you stock? Deliver it in person, and make a real impression. Have a customer expecting to receive those new clothes next week? Ship them overnight but don't charge them for overnight shipping.

What transpires during the actual delivery to let the customer know you're interested in more than just this single transaction? It may be simple things, like being timely or efficient, or producing accurate invoices. Or, it could be cause for celebration. You risk communicating the wrong messages when the order or delivery is not everything it should be; messages like "We're only interested in getting your money," or "We're only concerned about our service or product, not about you—the customer."

- Gauge how your delivery measures up with my suggested checklist (Exhibit 8.2). Identify opportunities to both improve communications with your customers, and to win over customers with impressive delivery.

Follow-Up Communication

For us, it's not just a question of how well your car performs day-to-day, but also how we perform as its maker. So, if it ever crossed your mind that our commitment will diminish over time—now that you've written the check and driven home—think again. If anything, now is when the real stuff begins.

Introduction at the beginning of the Saturn owner's handbook

Continuing to build a loyal customer relationship after the sale is the "real stuff," and obviously Saturn believes in it. In the last chapter, we looked at the first four steps of Saturn's "Six Steps To Customer Enthusiasm." Now we look at number five:

Follow up with the Customer to ensure that the Customer's expectations were met or exceeded.

Saturn recognizes that follow-up is a way to work smarter instead of harder. So much so, that it offers sales consultants a half-day advanced training course on follow-up.

Checklist For Delivery Procedures

Item	Most of the Time	Some-times	Almost Never
Order is complete	❏	❏	❏
Delivery time meets the customer's schedule	❏	❏	❏
Delivery method is convenient for the customer	❏	❏	❏
People handling the delivery are professional and efficient	❏	❏	❏
Invoices, statements, or packing lists are accurate	❏	❏	❏
Complete paperwork (instructions, warranties, etc.) is included	❏	❏	❏
Forms/info for placing future orders or accessories are included	❏	❏	❏
Customers are informed of easy ways to contact the company	❏	❏	❏
Customer assistance is available when the customer needs it	❏	❏	❏
Customers are thanked for their business	❏	❏	❏
Customers are impressed with delivery	❏	❏	❏
Customers say "WOW!" about the delivery	❏	❏	❏

Exhibit 8.2   Checklist for Delivery Procedures

So, what's the big deal about follow-up for Saturn? I believe it offers the company some advantages:

- It sets Saturn apart from the competition.

- Saturn finds out whether the customer is truly satisfied.

- Saturn shows that customer satisfaction is really important.

- It aids in preventing problems.

- Continued follow-up actually helps make Saturn's job easier in the long run.

"Oh yeah, right." I know that's what you're thinking about that last item. Yes, follow-up is hard work and a time commitment. How does it make Saturn's job easier in the long run? In a couple of ways. Within 12 months of purchasing a car, about 62 percent of customers will know of some family member or relative that purchases a car. That means more great word-of-mouth referrals. Another way it helps is because people move, people change positions, people talk to other people, conditions change, and people continue to meet new people. Keeping up with customers through follow-up opens the door to new opportunities in terms of increased sales. And future sales to existing customers will come with a higher profit margin.

Saturn considers follow-up so important that standards for this communication are established contractually with retailers. New owners are to be contacted at intervals of 3 days, 30 days, and 60 days after purchasing their cars. And at the retail level, my experience has been that they do indeed understand this importance and take it seriously. Experienced sales consultants have seen the value of follow-up. Fortunately, there are many ways to communicate after the sale, and Saturn makes good use of all of them.

They keep sending me stuff in the mail—it makes me feel like part of the family.

Linda Baldwin

It is important to note that the first follow-up immediately after the sale is a nonselling activity. The purpose is *not* to sell more products or services. Remember that creating loyal customers is all about long-term relationship-building.

Within a few days after purchasing my Saturn, I received a follow-up phone call from my sales consultant, and a thank you card with a hand-written note. Soon after that, I received a letter of thanks from the general manager of the retail facility. From then on, the mail campaign was full-speed ahead. Note, they do give customers fair warning. Early on, I received a flyer that stated the following on the outside: "Taking your Saturn home wasn't the end of your relationship with us." On the inside the flyer stated,

> As a matter of fact, it was the beginning. At Saturn, we make a point to stay in touch with our customers. You'll find we try to keep you posted on things we think might interest you. (We hope you'll do the same with us.)

Within one week after I purchased my Saturn, I received a call from the retailer's customer service liaison, wanting to know if I had any questions or problems. He then asked me several questions about how they performed in the selling and delivery process.

Less than a month after my purchase, I received the following items from the Saturn Team at Spring Hill:

- A thank-you postcard from a woman on the transmission team (see Exhibit 8.3)
- An emergency key for my Saturn
- A "Welcome to the family" cover letter and booklet full of useful information

A survey form on the purchase of my new Saturn arrived within a month (more on surveys shortly). It was accompanied

I'd like to thank you for buying a Saturn, and believing in us. When the first Saturn rolled off the assembly line in 1990, a lot of people thought we'd never succeed. Well, you proved them wrong, along with more than one million other Saturn owners.

It didn't take long for me to understand that Saturn is special. They encourage team spirit and sharing responsibilities so everyone has a real chance to contribute. It's nice because I know that my job on the transmission team is just as important as the job of an engineer who draws up the plans, or a retailer who owns the store. We all understand that there is a little bit of all of us in every car we build.

I hope you enjoy your Saturn. Every single piece of it.

Exhibit 8.3   Saturn Thank-You Postcard

by a letter from the retail facility, which once again thanked me for my purchase. Around the end of the first month came another follow-up phone call from my sales consultant.

And then came yet another letter of thanks. This time it was from the retail service and parts team—and with it came a $20 gift certificate for Saturn accessories or parts. (The gifts can vary: A friend who purchased a Saturn received a certificate for an oil change.)

When my car is due for service, I receive a nice, inviting reminder notice in the mail. After my first service, I received a "thanks for coming in" letter from the operations manager.

At Christmas time, I received a holiday card in the mail from my sales consultant. It contained a surprise—a photo of me and my new Saturn taken when I purchased the car. I can't wait until I've had my car for one year. Friends tell me they receive Happy Birthday cards from Saturn for their cars!

There have been additional communications, which you'll read about shortly. There is one more thing to note about Saturn's communications with me as a customer: They took various forms and came from various sources. Saturn Corporation has a binder full of preprinted cards, thank you notes, and all sorts of written communications that retailers can order. These materials have a consistent look and feel, and display the Saturn logo, so all bear a Saturn family resemblance. Retailers can elect to handle their own mailings in-house, or use the services of Saturn Customer Communications to manage mailing lists and these communications for them.

In a "different" turnabout, it is common for customers to SEND TO Saturn thank-you notes, cards, letters, and even poems and songs they have written about their car or their Saturn experience. Saturn retailers have binders or bulletin boards full of the stuff, where everybody (employees, prospects, and customers) can see them.

WHAT YOU CAN DO

Follow-Up Communication

- The importance of keeping in touch with customers really hit home with one real estate broker that I'll refer to as Dee. She told me about losing some addresses of her customers when she moved herself. Much later, Dee located the lost addresses and promptly mailed each person a note with a calendar. The very next day, she received a call from one of these past customers. The caller was so thankful, since she had lost Dee's phone number, and because she was ready to sell her house, AND because she had an appointment scheduled with another agent the next week, AND instead, could Dee please come over right away? Dee did, got the contract, sold the house, AND later sold that customer's mother's house and her sister's house.

- Of course, it can take time to see results from follow-up efforts. I know of an insurance and investment professional who calls customers and qualified prospects on their birthday, just to wish them a happy birthday. Sometimes they call back to say thanks for the call. Sometimes it jiggles their memory to bring up a change in their life—one that requires new or additional insurance or investments. One prospect that he had been calling faithfully for 10 years, just to say happy birthday, had just made a job change. In this case, the end result of follow-up was a new customer and a big chunk of business. So, stick with follow-up efforts. Take a look at what you can do based on the Saturn follow-up communication methods we just covered:

  Telephone. It's simple to use for follow-up, and probably the most widely-used method. A phone call can be effective for saying thanks, verifying satisfaction, and for reminders. If you have an aversion to phone recorders and voice mail, get over it. It is much better to have at least made the effort than to do nothing at all. Practice what you will say before you make the call. If you're leaving a message, be aware of your tone of voice, and speak clearly. Let the person you're calling know if any action is necessary on their part. If you want a return phone call, be sure to state that fact and to leave your phone number.

  Thank-you notes. They don't have to be elaborate, and your message only needs to be short and sweet. Cards that are printed or embossed with your company name and logo can look very professional. Don't lightly dismiss the value of handwritten thank-you notes. They really can make an impression. I once received a thank-you note from an unexpected source . . . my plumber! And, after I mentioned that fact when speaking to a local business audience, some people called wanting to know the identity of the plumber, so they could be customers also.

Greeting cards. Nowadays, there are greeting cards and holidays for just about everything imaginable. Some of the obvious are standard holidays and birthdays. Thanksgiving is a great time to say "thanks for your business." So is your customer's anniversary. No, not their wedding anniversary. Rather, the anniversary date of when they started doing business with you. Dare to be different. If you're an accountant who's been remiss about keeping in touch with some business clients, you might take advantage of Groundhog Day. Send a "Happy Groundhog Day" greeting, expressing the sentiment that you're finally emerging from your cubbyhole to check on their business future and welfare.

Personal letters/notes. Personal letters almost seem a thing of the past; maybe that's why they can still make an impact. The more personalized the letter is, the greater the personal impact. A form letter congratulating a customer on the purchase of a new car just doesn't compare to a letter addressing the customer by name and referring to their gold SL2 purchased three weeks ago. When you learn of something that might be of interest to a customer, business-wise or hobby-wise, drop them a note. Enclose a news article or magazine clipping.

Postcards. It's hard to miss the message when you don't have to open an envelope. Postcards can be used for reminders and thank you's, and even as greeting cards. Shortly after I received a questionnaire about my new Saturn purchase, I received a simple white postcard in the mail from Saturn. It served as a reminder for me to complete and return the survey, and a thanks for my valuable opinions.

The Communication Process Continues

A service event about basic mechanics of the car was great, gave me a greater appreciation for how the Saturn is designed, built, and serviced. I felt more confident about my car purchase.

Keith Hattwig

We kick in to a higher gear now with other types of communications after the sale, most of which encourage back-and-forth dialog with customers. These methods can also go both ways as an education process. Customers learn from Saturn, and Saturn learns from customers. And that's the way it should be in any business. In this section, we'll look at Saturn's new-owner workshops, the Customer Assistance Center, surveys, newsletters, and the Saturn web site.

Workshops or Seminars

They offered us classes on how to maintain our cars and showed us how to change the oil and our tire—and fed us dinner and gave out door prizes. All of which was free to us.

Patti & Mark Clum

The classes that Saturn customers Patti and Mark Clum referred to above are actually "Saturn New Owner Workshops." Most Saturn retailers host these on a regular basis. It's not uncommon for 60 to 80 people to attend one. I had noticed signs announcing the workshop schedules at the retail facility when I purchased my car. Then, shortly after my purchase, I received a letter inviting me to a workshop. The one I attended started off on a Saturday morning, under a tent, with coffee, juice, and donuts provided. My classmates were a mix of young and old, singles, couples, families, men and women. We were there to become familiar with our car, the retail facility, and team members. Even if we never intended to service the car ourselves, we would still learn some useful information—like keeping the warranty in effect and protecting our investment.

We customers were referred to as guests, and introduced to the Saturn service team members (technicians who were volunteering for this duty on their day off). Technicians worked with small groups of people, each gathered around a Saturn, to teach about some standard stuff like checking fluid levels, why it's important to change the oil regularly, what is where under the hood, how to safely change a tire. We saw underneath the car. A retail partner demonstrated the proper way to maintain the car's interior and exterior appearance. We got answers to our questions about warranties and service, and tips on using the right replacement fluids. Next came the fun stuff—drawings for lots of door prizes like key chains and coffee mugs, and the grand prize, a bucket full of car wash-and-wax products. Then everybody was treated to a catered barbecue lunch. (Food seems to be a common theme at Saturn events, and very popular with customers. But then again, if you were entertaining family or guests in your home, wouldn't food and refreshments be part of it?)

At the end, each person was presented with a frameable "Certificate of Recognition for attending the New Owners Workshop" (see Exhibit 8.4). And for our later use, we were given a folder with information including a neat "list of sounds used to describe car conditions." That should come in handy when we need to communicate with our service technicians! The folder also contained information on extended vehicle coverage plans, motor oil, general maintenance, the Saturn CarClub, and a short guest survey form for our completion. The retailer uses the feedback to make adjustments and improvements on the workshop. The form asked for our feedback on the workshop, with these questions:

- How did we [the retailer] do? (a low-to-high ranking by numbers 1, 2, 3, or 4)

- Was your Saturn New Owner Workshop too long, too short, or just right?

- What part of your Workshop did you find most useful?

- What can we do to improve your Workshop?

- Additional comments or suggestions you have for us

Exhibit 8.4   Saturn Certificate of Recognition

The end result is that workshops are one more step in building loyal customer relationships. Customers view them as a great form of communication, where they can learn, have a little fun, enjoy good food, and meet other customers. For Saturn, it's a learning experience also, as team members hear comments and receive feedback. And it's an investment in customer loyalty.

WHAT YOU CAN DO

Workshops or Seminars

- In this case, I am referring to seminars or workshops designed for existing customers, not necessarily to attract new customers. What's the difference between a seminar and workshop? Maybe not much. A seminar is usually "a meeting for an exchange of ideas." A workshop implies more "hands-on" or active participation.

- These seminars or workshops should be used primarily as a communication tool, and not to make money by selling more products or services (although that can result). Look to give information of value and interest to your customers, and to establish a working comfort level.

- How can you do something similar to Saturn's new-owner workshops for your business? Consultants, investment counselors, and even attorneys now use brief seminars to familiarize existing clients with new laws or services that may have some impact and benefit for clients. Retail stores hold seminars to help customers learn how to use their products. Industrial equipment manufacturers team up with distributors for the same purpose.

- What is it that you have to communicate to customers? Present the information in an easy-to-understand way. Keep it interesting and entertaining. Detailed technoblab can be very B-O-R-I-N-G, so make sure that you have an excellent presenter who can lighten things up. Demonstrate products. Make the seminar or workshop as interactive as possible. Let customers see, touch, feel, or otherwise experience it. Help make customers feel like a part of it, as in "We're in this together for the betterment of each other." Sharing inside information lets customers know how special they are. Let them know about new products and services before they're available to the general public.

- Have an appreciation for your customer's busy schedule, and keep the seminar length appropriate, while providing as much value as possible. Set aside some time for discussion and feedback, and have customers complete an evaluation form. Afterward, have a drawing, give some token gifts, offer special sales, discounts, or perks, or find some other appropriate way to thank customers for participating. Don't forget the food and refreshments! And remember what I said about making money by selling more products or services? At the end of the new-owner workshop that I attended, the retailer opened up the parts department for customers to purchase accessories at a special discount. Customers were by now a little more aware of the existence and benefits of certain accessories, and were appreciative of the discount they were being offered that day. (Can't you just hear that cash register ringing? Cha-Ching!)

Customer Assistance Centers

So what happens if you're a Saturn customer, you don't care to attend a workshop, but you still have questions or comments? Not to worry. It's Saturn's Customer Assistance Center to the rescue. The Center consists of about 110 team members, in different capacities, working out of Spring Hill. They are focused with their own mission statement:

To generate Customer and Team Member enthusiasm by incorporating practices throughout the Customer Assistance Center that focus on understanding Customer and Team Member needs, and identifying opportunities to exceed their expectations.

Remember my version of the customer loyalty wheel in Chapter 3? Well, the Customer Assistance Center has its own version, revolving around three elements: team member enthusiasm, customer enthusiasm, and increased profitability. The structure of the center is two-tiered. The first tier consists of the owner communication team (OCT) and the customer support consultants (CSC).

The OCTs handle all incoming mail from owners, which can amount to between 1,500 and 3,000 pieces of correspondence each month. All mail is scanned into a computer and stored electronically. About 65 percent of that correspondence requires some kind of response, and the goal of the center is to generate a verbal or written response within 3 days for letters, or 24 hours for e-mail.

The CSCs handle all incoming calls to the center's toll-free number, which range from a whopping 17,000 to 30,000 per month. However, unlike the centers at many large companies where the majority of calls relate to problems or complaints, a high 65 percent of the calls to Saturn's center are information seeking calls. Many are calls that can be answered on the spot, like, "What kind of oil should I use in my Saturn?" More involved calls that require some type of additional response might be something like, "I have 50,000 miles on my car and the alternator just failed, and I think Saturn should pay to replace it." The center responds to the customer the same day or no later than the close of business the next business day, either with a resolution to the problem or at least an acknowledgment of the problem. The problem situations that can't be answered immediately advance to the center's second tier.

The Customer Assistance Center's second tier consists of teams of customer assistance managers (CAMs), who handle approximately 4,000 cases each month and 950 pieces of owner correspondence per month. A case is opened for the more problematic situations, like the one involving a failed alternator. Exactly how cases are handled is explained in the next chapter on solving problems.

What enables these team members at the center to communicate effectively with customers? It starts with hiring quality people, who must first go through a behavioral interview, then team interviews. In the behavioral interview, Saturn looks for attributes such as these:

- Effective spoken communication skills

- Perceptive to customer needs

- Strong decision-making skills

- Ability to cope with challenging situations

- Team-oriented

- Solid commitment to task responsibilities

Once quality people are hired (by consensus decision making, of course), initial training begins. I'm sure that comes as no surprise to you at this point. CSCs are trained on roles and responsibilities, Saturn history, products, programs, warranties, customer handling, case documentation, and systems overviews. CAMs are trained on roles and responsibilities, managing customer expectations, program policies and procedures, warranty, vehicle policy and goodwill, and case documentation. Continuous training takes the form of team meetings, Customer Assistance Center meetings, Saturn training classes, and field visits to retailers.

Knowledgeable team members, structured systems, and technology combine to make the Customer Assistance Center a responsive and easy way for customers to communicate with Saturn. And it's one more great way for Saturn to take the customers' pulses and to continue building those long-term relationships.

WHAT YOU CAN DO

Customer Assistance Centers

Here we're talking about centers or departments that are designed to accommodate existing customers, not centers for taking new orders.

- Once again, start with a qualified, trained staff. Yes, it may be difficult. But you've probably heard the statement that it takes months to find a customer and seconds to lose one. A new customer who needs information or assistance may be gone in seconds—if that first call for help is met by someone that is not helpful.

- Use the best equipment and technology possible to accommodate the workload, to make it easy for your staff, and to make it fast for your customers.

- Establish reasonable standards for handling and response, but concentrate on quality, not quantity.

- Keep customers informed. If you can't provide the information or answers right away, let the customers know when they can expect to hear back from you. Don't ask the *customers to call you* back. They already called; they're now communicating with you and it's your turn to take the initiative. Although the CSCs at Saturn's Customer Assistance Center are expected to return calls no later than the close of the next business day, that doesn't necessarily mean that they have answers for the customers. Even if they don't have the answer, the call is still made within the time frame to let the customer know what's going on.

Surveys

Not long after purchasing a Saturn car (usually within one to three weeks) each customer receives a questionnaire form in the mail. Saturn really values this customer feedback. A brief introduction at the beginning of the form explains that "our goal is to provide *complete* customer satisfaction with our products, facilities and services." Questions relate to Saturn performance in the following five areas:

- Your retailer's sales team
- Your retailer's facility
- Paying for your Saturn
- Delivery
- Overall Saturn Experience

Possible responses range across five levels, from "not at all satisfied" to "completely satisfied." The questionnaire ends with a note of thanks, along with a toll-free 800 number for the Saturn Customer Assistance Center. A self-addressed, postage-paid envelope is included for return of the questionnaire. (In other words, Saturn makes it easy for customers to respond!)

Some Saturn service customers may receive a similar survey form within one to three weeks of taking their car in for service. This survey form focuses questions in four areas:

- Your retailer's service team
- Your retailer's service work

- Saturn service in general

- Your overall Saturn Experience

Saturn does a fantastic job with its customer communication surveys, getting responses from nearly 60 percent of sales recipients and 35 percent of service recipients. Designing surveys and measuring customer satisfaction can be a tricky business. Saturn spent about a year revising its new-owner survey. To do so, it incorporated inputs from field people, retailers, a franchise operation team, and a customer experiences task force. The revised survey is basically designed to measure three areas: performance to standards, specific behaviors, and the willingness of customers to recommend Saturn (good old word-of-mouth exposure). The survey results are used to develop loyalty in a more global sense, by helping Saturn and its retailers on a local, regional, and national basis. Reports showing performance against standards are shared monthly with retail and field people. Of course, the true test is whether customers come back for service or another purchase.

Saturn makes use of surveys for other purposes, too—like market research, or the guest survey for workshops. But what all of these surveys do is help customers talk to Saturn. Decisions are not made at Saturn based on what people inside Saturn think only they know. "What do customers think about this?" is the question most likely heard around Saturn, and surveys are one way of determining the answers.

WHAT YOU CAN DO

Surveys

Businesses must continually ask customers questions like: "How are we doing? What do you like or dislike about our business? How can we better serve you?" Why should *you* bother to ask these questions? Two reasons: (1) you need continuous improvement in order to survive; and (2) a typical business hears from only 4 percent of its dissatisfied customers. The other 96 percent just go quietly away, and 91 percent of them will never come back. If you don't know that a problem exists, or what the problem is, you will not have the opportunity to correct and improve. You risk the loss of what could have been very loyal customers. You risk the loss of profitable business. Surveys or questionnaires are one way to ask the important questions.

- Questionnaires or surveys can take many different forms, from a simple three-question postcard to a complicated multipage check-the-box form, and can be conducted by mail, in person, or by phone. If you're not sure what will work for your business, try a few different methods on a small test group of customers. Or treat a couple of customers to a cup of coffee or lunch, and ask them just three key questions, like the how and what questions mentioned earlier. Then, sit back and listen.

- I was in a doughnut shop (part of a national chain) when I noticed a stack of flyers on the counter. Just one-half page in length, these flyers bore the headline "We'd Love To Hear From You!!" This minisurvey invited customers to call the chain's toll-free phone number and "share with us how you feel about any of these topics." (Hint: Make it easy to respond.) It listed six areas—things like "how well we served you" and "what you liked or disliked about our coffee." (Hint: Keep it simple.) It then went on to explain that "when you call, our operators will listen to what you say and ask you a couple of additional questions. They'll report to us what you have to say, so we can make things better for everyone." (Hint: Listen and use the information.) In closing they offered "to send you some special coupons for more doughnuts." (Hint: Encourage/reward customers to respond.)

- Don't overdo it with surveys. Some people just won't be bothered with them. You definitely can't expect to get anywhere close to a 100 percent return. Measuring survey results can be difficult, and further complicating the issue is the fact that customer attitudes shift frequently. You may not get the real picture, or you may get a different picture at a different time. So don't base everything solely on satisfaction surveys. Remember, a satisfied customer is not necessarily a loyal customer. Make an effort also to track repurchase loyalty, and you just might discover whether customers are speaking out by buying more, less, or not at all.

Newsletters

Saturn retailers each do their own thing with customer newsletters. Some prepare them in-house, others use outside agencies. Some are published monthly, others are published bimonthly or quarterly. Saturn of Louisville has an attractive bimonthly publication (see Exhibit 8.5). One large sheet is folded down to a 10-by-14-inch, 4-page newsletter, printed in 4 colors on the outside and 2 colors on the inside. A recent issue included how-to information, like towing your Saturn behind a recreational vehicle, keeping your car cool, and getting it ready for summer. It also had some information about car accessories and fun stuff, and included a special service offer coupon—for Saturns only. In addition to these types of features, there are certain items that are normally included in each issue:

- Business hours for sales, service, and parts
- Web site address and complete facility address and phone number
- Used-car gallery

SATURN OF LOUISVILLE

SATURN — A DIFFERENT KIND OF COMPANY. A DIFFERENT KIND OF CAR.

April 1998

A GIFT FROM THE HEART

Donor drive gave Valentine's Day gift to the nation

What better way to say "I love you" than with roses? For Saturn dealerships across the country on Valentine's Day, the answer was the gift of life.

Give the Gift of Life
National Donor Day
February 14, 1998 © Valentines Day

In a cooperative effort with United Auto Workers Spring Hill Local 1853, Saturn Corporation and its retailers sponsored the first-ever National Donor Day on Feb. 14. Saturn saw 100 percent cooperation from its 380 dealerships across the country, including Saturn of Louisville. Around 9,000 individuals participated.

"It was an unprecedented coalition of blood, tissue and organ donor agencies that got together to help save lives," said Greg Martin, Saturn spokesperson. The blood collection alone of about 8,000 units, he said, may be the largest one-day blood collection in American history.

Those attending had several options for sharing the gift of life with others. They could donate blood and platelets; pledge to donate organs and tissues as well as bone marrow; and learn about donating umbilical cord blood, which is rich in special disease-fighting cells.

"It was a very upbeat atmosphere," said Lavona Casey, Saturn of Louisville sales manager, who coordinated our donor drive. "Everybody had a good feeling about what was happening and it felt good to be participating."

American Red Cross representatives were on hand at Saturn of Louisville to share smiles and provide information. Blood donors were treated to snacks and refreshments, and organ donors received stress-relieving hand cushions shaped like hearts.

Blood has a limited shelf life, so the supply has to be constantly replenished. The various donations from National Donor Day will not only be used in emergency rooms and intensive care units, but will also benefit victims of leukemia, aplastic anemia, severe burns, immune disorders and other life-threatening conditions.

Our participation in National Donor Day, just like our volunteer program to build playgrounds in areas of need, goes back to the Saturn philosophy of getting involved in our own backyard. "We like to give back to the community," Lavona said.

Thanks to all who joined us for this life-enriching event. If you'd like to reach out to others through our Saturn CarClub chapter, call Joan Lawrence or Linda Parker at (502) 499-5060. And we hope to see you here next year for the next National Donor Day!

Donor questions — and answers — were in abundance at the National Donor Day event.

A cold glass of orange juice helps to replenish a blood donor's fluids.

A donor is carefully monitored by a Red Cross representative.

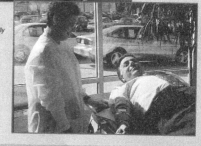

HOW TO PRESERVE LIFE

For more information on being a donor, contact the following:
Blood and platelet donations — America's Blood Centers at 1-888-BLOOD-88 (toll-free), or the American Red Cross at 1-800-GIVE-LIFE.
Bone marrow and umbilical cord donations — National Marrow Donor Program at 1-800-MARROW-2.
Organ and tissue donation — Transplant Recipients International Organization at 1-800-TRIO-386, or the Coalition on Donation at 1-800-355-SHARE.

Exhibit 8.5   Saturn of Louisville Newsletter

- Schedules for the new-owner workshops
- A select Saturn car model article
- An article about what Saturn is doing in the community
- A retail team member spotlight article
- A customer story

Saturn of Louisville customers receive their newsletters by mail, and plenty of extra copies are available in the showroom. Customers have told me how much they enjoy receiving the newsletter, and how it continues to make them feel connected to their Saturn family.

Saturn used to produce a quarterly newsletter for national distribution to all customers, but that eventually became the *Connector,* a quarterly newsletter for members of the Saturn CarClub. It's a large, folded 4-page newsletter that's fun and informative, with, of course, lots of customer stories. (You can read more about the CarClub in Chapter 10.) A recent issue included the following articles:

- "100,000 Tales"—stories from Saturn owners whose cars have hit the 100,000-mile mark
- "Under the Hood (A to Z)"—a series providing facts about your Saturn (this one dealing with air bags)
- "Good Deeds"—a continuing series celebrating the very good things Saturn CarClubs do
- "Road Recounts"—stories of Saturn CarClubbers road trips
- "Best Saturn Moment"—letter from a CarClubber
- "Scrub a Dub Dub"—pointers for washing your Saturn
- "2 Sum Up"—fun facts and figures about Saturn Car-Clubbers

- "Your Color Horoscope"—horoscopes for owners, based on the color of their Saturn. For example:

   Grey Bronze—Why choose a color that everyone else has? You like to keep people guessing. Never too revealing, there are many different sides to your personality. Not only are you down to earth, you are also somewhat of a dreamer. Our advice to you? Try exploring your artistic side.

The back of the *Connector* included an easy-to-use cut-out form, inviting customers to submit their own stories, photos, feature ideas, or letters to the editor.

Internally, Saturn Corporation produces a variety of newsletters for supplier partners, retail partners, CarClub coordinators, and team members. All of these newsletters contain information that eventually helps team members communicate more effectively with customers. When everybody in the company is kept informed and the information is shared, customers end up better informed.

WHAT YOU CAN DO

Newsletters

- It seems like LOTS of businesses use newsletters these days to communicate. With PCs and desktop-publishing-made-easy programs, even Aunt Ida can publish a 4-page newsletter every Christmas. The main objective of a newsletter for customers is to provide them with information. But if that is your *only* use of a newsletter, you're missing the boat.

- Newsletters can be used as a vehicle to encourage two-way communication. Include a survey form or question, a contest entry form, coupons, or some way to get customers to talk back to you. Newsletters can help introduce customers to the array of products and services that you have to offer, and announce new ones. You can use stories and customer testimonials to demonstrate the benefits of your products and services. And for customers that speak with your employees but never have a chance to meet them, you can put faces together with names through an employee spotlight feature and photo.

- Newsletters can range from plain to fancy, from short to long, from small to oversize, and from one to full color. You have lots of decisions to make when it comes to producing newsletters. Should it be produced in-house, or by an outside firm? How much time should you devote to it? How often should it be published? Make your plans and budget commitments in advance. Keep in mind when budgeting that a newsletter is just one of many forms of communication available. If you choose to go ahead, stick with it for a justifiable time period. I've heard from quite a few companies that when they decided to discontinue their customer newsletter, or were late to release an issue, customers would start calling to ask what happened. Hopefully, that's a sign that customers look forward to reading the newsletter, and that they value it as a communication tool.

Web Sites

By now, you're probably beginning to notice that Saturn's web site is useful in many different areas. Here are a few ways that Saturn continues the communication process with Internet-using customers after the sale.

CarClub—owners can get the scoop on joining the club, and can read a few articles from the club's latest issue of the *Connector* newsletter

Letters to Saturn—read a few of the letters from other Saturn customers

Frequently Asked Questions—check out car care and maintenance tips

Photo Opportunity—see other Saturn customers posing with their cars, or submit your own photo

E-mail Saturn—once again, an opportunity to communicate one-to-one by submitting your comments or questions electronically

In the future, Saturn hopes to set up even more ways for customers to talk with them, like special chat events. However, in the meantime, there's plenty to do and see—and ways to communicate—at Saturn's web site.

WHAT YOU CAN DO
Web Sites

- Include relevant information and pages for existing customers. If you're not sure just what that might be, talk to a few of your Internet-savvy customers and ask them what they'd like to see on your web site.

- Invite two-way communication with some interactive activities, like chat sessions; real-time interviews; or a question of the week, with responses. I remember hearing about one good-size company that broadcast their annual shareholders' meeting live over the Internet, accessible at their web site. Computer users could see and hear company officials, and e-mail questions for possible answering during the meeting.

- At a minimum, include e-mail connections. You can even (cautiously) use e-mail to send customers thank-you notes, surveys, reminders, and newsletters. Did you know that you can even send cyber-thanks (flowers, meals, gifts, etc.) to customers via e-mail? Not the real thing, but a picture of your "gift." After you have visited the appropriate web site and made your selection, the recipient is notified via e-mail that a gift from you awaits them at a certain address, and they are supplied with a code number to access and view their gift.

- Provide phone numbers, addresses, customer assistance and other contact information on one page, making clear to customers the other ways they can communicate with you. And don't forget to advertise your web site address to your customers on all of your company literature.

Special Things That "Reach Out and Touch"

As I interviewed Saturn customers, it became apparent that the "little things" were what stuck out in their minds as something special. Not that I was surprised. After all, when I count my blessings at the end of the day, it's all the little things that add up. And so it is with long-term customer relationships. It's another way of communicating that you care after the sale.

One businessperson told me about her routine of sending birthday cards to customers. She was seriously thinking about discontinuing the practice, until she received a call of thanks from an elderly female client. Seems it was the only birthday card this client received; she didn't even get one from her family. The client was deeply touched that someone else would remember and care.

A Saturn retailer told me about a practice that seems to be much appreciated by customers. About two weeks after purchasing their car, customers find on their doorstep a Saturn "Snack Pack," containing a coffee mug and chocolate chip cookies.

(Observation: cookie lovers sure seem to be common among customers!)

There are no policies or requirements at Saturn for doing these little things. It's all part of the Saturn culture and values. Sometimes retailers and sales consultants exchange information about what's worked for them. Sometimes it's just somebody's neat idea of the right thing to do. Sometimes the cost is out of a sales consultant's own pocket. Whatever the case, it's another element in the customer loyalty process.

Here are a few examples of special things that reached out and touched me as a Saturn customer:

- When I picked up my new car, my sales consultant gave me a bag containing Saturn cup holders and a bottle of touch-up paint for the car.

- The car had a full tank of gas when I picked it up.

- Then, when I went to fill up with gas about a week later, I couldn't help but smile when I opened the gas port door. In a slot inside the door was a note from my sales consultant that read, "Hope you are enjoying your Saturn," and it was signed with a smiley face.

I'm going to let Saturn customers speak in the rest of this section. They will describe for you what reached out and touched them.

One nice thing they do is wash your car when they're done with service, and they leave the inside as clean as it was when you bring it in. And they usually have free cookies. The main thing Saturn does that other businesses should do is treat customers with respect. It's like we're (Saturn owners) part of a club or family of sorts. This may sound strange, but I actually LIKE taking my car into Saturn for stuff.

Eric Penn

They took a picture of me standing by my new car. I felt very proud and very confident that I had made the right choice. Later, they posted a picture of me and my car in the showroom for everyone to see.

Renee Minges

My sales consultant called and said his licensing clerk informed him that it would be possible to transfer my existing specialty license plate from my trade-in car to the new car, saving me a little money. They didn't have to do that. It made me feel they were watching out for me.

Lynn Smith

They enlarged the photo of me standing next to my new Saturn, and put it on a wall calendar. I have it hanging up in my office, where everybody can see it.

Linda Bader

I purchased a used Saturn. Later, I received a letter from the Saturn folks at Spring Hill, asking if there was anything they could do to help me and my Saturn get better acquainted.

Brad Houts

I took the car in for them to touch up a tiny scratch, and wanted to get it washed, but the person who washed wasn't there, so our salesman washed it himself.

Charles Chamberlain

They practically kissed me when I bought the car. I've had two purple cars. They even sent me a purple T-shirt to match my car.

Roger Burns

The reason I feel like part of the Saturn family is that, for one thing, they know who you are when you walk in the door. I always feel welcome. I also like getting invitations to open houses, service seminars, and lots of special treatment.

Lynn Holberton

They call after I have anything done to the car.

Thelma McKinney

I hope hearing from these Saturn customers helps you generate some "What You Can Do" ideas for your own business. However, one more word of caution is in order here: *sincerity.* If these special little things are not done as a sincere part of the way you do business, they can appear to be gimmicky marketing ploys. And that will *not* make for loyal customers.

WOW CUSTOMERS WITH FOLLOW-UP

Think of how hard you've worked to get customers. You have invested time, effort, and dollars. Don't let everything go down the drain because of lack of communication and follow-up after the sale. Take a fresh look at your delivery process, follow-up methods, and frequency and effectiveness of communications. Use a variety of communication methods, and consider it an ongoing process. Provide easy ways for customers to talk back to you. Strive to make communication a true two-way process, and learn from your customers. "WOW" your customers with special little things that can make a difference in building long-term relationships.

9

Solve Problems

"I Need Some Help"

I took my wife's '97 SC2 in today for the recall. BEFORE I could even call to make the appointment, the retailer had called and left a message to inform me of the recall. They said they were scanning the computer and calling all who should have received the recall notice! Anyway, as promised, they had the work completed within one hour. When I went to pick up my car, I was surprised to find a Saturn Car Care Kit sitting in the car. I went back to ask why, and was informed it was a token for having to bring the car in for this recall!

Al Clapsaddle

The need for recalls on Saturns is pretty rare, but when Saturn announced its own voluntary recall on some 1997 models, it did so in the true Saturn way. Owners of affected cars received the recall notice from Saturn via FedEx overnight priority letter, with a free 20-minute phone card thrown in for good measure!

Just as personal relationships are not "wine and roses" all the time, neither are company and customer relationships. Problems happen. And when they happen in *your* business, what occurs and how are problems resolved? Situations when a customer has a problem should be viewed as an opportunity to gain a truly loyal customer. How you approach these problems, or strive to prevent them, can make all the difference in the world.

According to a J.D. Power & Associates Special Report (November 1996), more than 60 percent of all Saturn owners had no problems at all with their new sedans, wagons, and coupes during the first three months of ownership. When problems did occur, the resolution efforts were good enough to place Saturn among the top five in the industry in problem resolution, outperforming such nameplates as Lexus, Toyota, Honda, and Lincoln.

The actual need to solve problems will also occur during earlier stages of the buying process—not just after the sale. Look up *problem* in a thesaurus and you'll find words like *obstacle, predicament, challenge, snag, question,* and *confusion.* Salespeople are familiar with these words. In fact, they will tell you that these are what they face in their jobs on a daily basis. However, true sales professionals know that if they can offer a solution to a problem, they will make the initial sale and gain a customer. So don't operate on the mistaken assumption that the task of creating loyal customers by solving problems only occurs after the sale. Instead, continually be on the lookout for these challenges and opportunities!

Are you going to solve every problem to the delight of the customer? Obviously, no. Understand that sometimes it's okay to "agree to disagree," especially if the customer's demand is unreasonable. Like the customer that felt that he shouldn't have to pay the $400 transmission repair bill—for a car with 250,000 miles on it! Can you imagine? Yes, I suspect you can, because you've probably faced similar unreasonable requests yourself. In a tongue-in-cheek letter to Saturn, one couple wrote about having had their new Saturn for one month, with just one problem:

"We can't complain." They went on to explain that in the last 30 years they have had 12 new automobiles, and always had complaints. Seems it wasn't any fun if they had nothing to complain about.

Wouldn't it be nice if none of your customers ever complained? Don't smile at that thought too long, because the correct answer is "No." If you're not aware of customer problems, chances are your "Hear No Evil, See No Evil" approach is resulting in customers pouring out of the hole in the bottom of the leaky bucket. And you're losing out on the opportunity to gain genuinely loyal customers.

> *They earned my loyalty because they are loyal to me. They have won my trust and they are honest. They follow up as soon as possible on any problem that I have. I can leave my problems in their hands.*
>
> Maria Hutzler

Bad News Travels Faster Than a Souped-Up Coupe

Here are the top three reasons why it is important to solve problems for customers:

1. *Bad:* A typical dissatisfied customer will tell 8 to 10 people about his or her problem. One in 5 customers will tell 20 other people.

2. *Better:* Seven out of 10 complaining customers will do business with you again if you resolve the complaint in their favor.

3. *Best:* Solving problems for customers is the right thing to do. Don't friends rely on friends when they have problems?

Practice Preventive Maintenance

In the manufacturing process, Saturn realizes that if it relies only on inspections to assure quality, it's only fixing problems after they have occurred. So, Saturn focuses most on avoiding them in the first place, following a team-based quality system (described in Chapter 5).

The best course of action in problem solving is trying to prevent problems from developing in the first place. The second-best course is to prevent similar problems from repeating themselves. Third, when problems occur anyway, the best option is to execute a practiced attack, and go for the gold! Going for the gold in this case means cementing that loyal customer relationship. You're not going to win all of the time. Besides, your customers are on the same team with you anyway, so you strive to be a team and "win" together.

Saturn was faced with a scary problem early in its history, just a short ten months into production. One of their suppliers for engine coolants misformulated a batch. Instead of cooling, it ate the hoses, the water pump, and then the engine. Did Saturn elect to punt? No, the offense stayed on the field! Saturn sent letters to approximately 25,000 owners by registered mail, informing them whether their car was affected. Owners of each of the 1,836 affected cars were given a choice: a brand new car, identical to the one they owned, or return of the full purchase price to them. Very few asked for their money back, but about 98 percent said they had never been treated like that before, and willingly accepted Saturn's offer of a brand-new car. Then, Saturn rented a car crusher and, one by one, supervised destruction of the affected cars.

This is a great example of preventive maintenance. Instead of waiting to see whether the problem would occur, Saturn took the initiative. And it kept customers and helped create loyalty in the process.

Another way that Saturn practices true preventive maintenance is evident in its used car program. Every qualified used
car undergoes an extensive, 150-point-plus inspection. (Hint:
Subject your products and services to a great quality control
program BEFORE they are delivered to customers.) The inspection starts with an exterior look at the car. Then service team
members pop the hood and check fluid levels. Next, they
inspect the operation and condition of all the various lights and
turn signals. Then they test-drive the car under a wide range of
driving conditions. After the test-drive, many more vehicle
components get checked out before proceeding to the service
stall inspection. That's where things like the engine, brakes, and
tires are inspected. After all is said and done, Saturn takes two
more steps to help customers understand its commitment to
preventing problems. First, Saturn provides a limited warranty
and a 3-day money-back guarantee. Second, since a customer
may need a few weeks to feel really comfortable with his or her
purchase, Saturn throws in a 30-day/1,500-mile trade-in policy.

*Okay, here's why I'm driving my second Saturn, and when its
lease runs out in two years, I'm planning to order my third Saturn. :-) For me, the key is being treated like a human being at
the service department.*

E-mail from "Ericd"
*For the uninitiated e-mail users,
this :-) is a smiley face—look at
it sideways.*

Of course, you don't want bad things to happen, but when
they do, you need to be able to take care of them effectively. For
example, when customers have a problem with their Saturn,
even if they hate to bring it in, Saturn still hopes they will appreciate fast and effective service. Saturn prepares for this in some
of the same ways you should prepare in your business: through
employee training and communications. Here we go again on

training, but of course this is another Saturn difference—and an important part of preventive maintenance. Just like the consultative sales process, Saturn believes in and trains for the consultative service process. It views it as an extension of handling customers in its no-hassle, understanding sales approach. Saturn's three-and-one-half-day "Consultative Service Workshop" helps service consultants to:

- Reinforce communication and behavioral skills to make the Saturn Difference

- Comprehend the importance of teamwork and how to effectively communicate with customers and other team members

- Understand and practice the consultative service process

- Manage stress and time more effectively on the service team

- Identify opportunities for continuous improvement within their service area and to improve service effectiveness

- Handle customer complaints and understand the dynamics of the Saturn Customer Assistance Center

- Utilize the policy and procedures manual to understand the key points and intent

Saturn supplies the traditional support services for repair technicians, such as manuals and literature. Then it provides an extra service that aids in communication: a toll-free technical line that goes straight from the retail service facility to the experts at Saturn. Communication and effectiveness are enhanced with a satellite communication system that links Saturn to its retail facilities. This leads to an organized and fast parts-ordering and delivery system. After all, as a customer, don't you have high expectations that the part necessary to fix your product will be there when you need it? That's why Saturn's objective, when it comes to parts, is 100 percent availability. Nothing less is satisfactory.

Have you ever owned a car—or any consumer product—that has been involved in a major recall? How did you find out about the recall? Chances are that you read about it in the morning newspaper or saw it on the TV evening news. Now, when you have news to share with your family and close friends, how do you prefer they find out? Probably not via the grapevine or public notice. You want them to hear it from you first and personally. Note yet another way that Saturn practices preventive maintenance—through fast and proactive communication directly with customers, before it's news to the rest of the world. Notifications to customers about recalls are sent via overnight mail, to arrive before or at the time public notification is made. And what's even nicer is that customers with nonaffected cars (same model but not part of the recall) are also notified. Some retailers even place phone calls to customers, like they did for Al—the customer who was quoted at the beginning of this chapter.

Saturn also tries to make it easy for customers to practice preventive maintenance on their cars. Certain parts on the cars are color-coded to make servicing easier, no matter who does the servicing. I trust Saturn to do the servicing on my car, and I received in the mail a Saturn maintenance book for my first year. There's a section for each 3-month or 3,000-mile interval, which lists the recommended service. It also provides space for the service consultant to sign once it's done. That makes it easy for me to keep a history of my car care. After the last time I had my car serviced, I found a thank-you postcard on the dashboard (see Exhibit 9.1).

I see that as a nice touch—and further evidence of preventive maintenance. The service department wants to make sure I'm completely satisfied—that small problems are solved before they turn into big problems that could have been prevented.

Most customers never meet the people behind the scenes. I'd like to take this opportunity to thank you for choosing Saturn of Louisville and believing in our service department. My name is Robert Frost. I'm the Technician who worked on your car today. I take great pride in my work and in the Saturn product. If, *for any reason,* you are not completely satisfied with the service you received or cannot recommend this service department to a friend, <u>please</u> let your service consultant know about it. Your feedback will help us to continually improve and make your next visit event better!

> Thank You!
> Robert Frost
> Technician #46

Saturn of Louisville
#2 Swope Auto Center • Louisville, KY 40299 • (502) 499-3800

Exhibit 9.1   Saturn of Louisville Thank-You Card

Saturn's service departments—and services *you* provide after the sale—play important roles in preventive maintenance. No matter how good the buying process was, it can be quickly overshadowed by a bad service department experience. Then the opportunity to build loyal customer relationships is lost.

Tom and Ray Magliozzi answer car questions on a National Public Radio program and in their weekly syndicated newspaper column called "Click and Clack Talk Cars."[8] A letter once appeared in their newspaper column, from a very unhappy customer. Seems this customer took his car to a dealership for recall work, and also decided to get an oil change. (Of course, we are NOT talking about a Saturn car or retailer.) When the service people called to tell the customer that his car was ready, they told him that they had also topped off the windshield-wiper fluid. At this point, the customer was happy and even thrilled to think that the dealership was really taking care of him, since he hadn't even asked to have the windshield-washer fluid checked. When he picked up the car, he learned just how well his "buddies" had taken care of him—by charging him $6.36 for washer fluid. Now, if you're familiar with Tom and Ray, you know that they had a field day with this letter. Their final hope was that the dealership owner would have an epiphany, and say "Hey, why am I jeopardizing this customer's loyalty to make a lousy six extra bucks?"

WHAT YOU CAN DO

Practice Preventive Maintenance

- Do it right the first time. Eliminate defects in products and errors in service through quality control programs. Have a system in place to monitor and maintain quality control, and strive to push the bar higher. Audit your services as a quality control measure, and remember that it is a continuous process.

- Alert customers to problems that could develop, and provide solutions. For example, through new-owner workshops (discussed in Chapter 8), Saturn educates customers about problems that could develop if they do not practice preventive maintenance on their car, like changing the oil. To help make it easy for customers to remember, Saturn sends postcard reminders when their car is due for service. (And of course this helps Saturn get the service business.)

- Listen to customers. Play detective and search for clues of potential problems during conversations. Ward off those potential problems by providing helpful comments or information to the customer, or if the problem is internal, to the appropriate person within the company.

- Listen to employees. They are in the best position to make preventive maintenance suggestions because they are either close to the customer, or affected because it involves their particular job.
- Provide easy ways for customers to voice their concerns, and provide easy ways for employees to relay potential problems, without fear of being the "bearer of bad news."
- Learn from problems already encountered. Get to the root of the problem; don't just treat the symptoms.
- Fix it right the first time!
- Service after the sale is a factor whether you manufacture or distribute products, or if your business IS providing services. The following four questions to apply to your business will help you practice preventive maintenance, so you can excel with service:

    1. *What various services do you provide?* Make a list of services that are provided after the sale. Include the services for which you charge the customer a fee, and related services that are "free" for the customer. Saturn retailers, for example, provide fee-based automotive services, and Saturn also provides free roadside assistance.

    2. *What services do you charge for?* Now look at your list of services and put an asterisk next to those for which the customer is charged directly. Does it make sense to charge for these services, or are you risking a bad impression with customers? What's reasonable and fair? Saturn believes it's reasonable and fair to stand behind their products by providing free 24-hour roadside assistance throughout the term of a car's bumper-to-bumper warranty. Say you're a consultant who has just mailed a report to a client, then the client

calls later with ten minutes worth of questions about the report. Do you charge for those ten minutes?

3. *Is it easy for customers to access your services?* Why offer services if customers don't know about them or can't access them when they need to? Most Saturn retailers help make it easy for customers to remember when their car is due for routine service by sending postcard reminders. Saturn also provides toll-free phone numbers, and plenty of printed materials promote these numbers. The 24-hour assistance number appears where customers will likely need it, on the spare key holder, and on printed materials that owners keep in their car's glove box. Saturn wouldn't leave its best friends stranded. Do you? If you sold office furniture, would you just deliver the furniture to your customers' front door, and make them move it from there? If you provide products or services that most customers would use on evenings or weekends, is your customer assistance line only staffed on weekdays and during regular working hours?

4. *How well are you providing these services?* How are you going to know if you don't ask? Saturn retailers sometimes call customers after they've had their car in for an oil change or service. They're curious to know if service was provided to the customer's satisfaction, or if there are any problems. Even my veterinarian calls the day after my dog has had her shots, to make sure she's doing okay. I know of a hair salon that employs a customer-service rep to call patrons a few days after their visit. This salon owner recognizes that some customers won't express dissatisfaction directly to their stylist, but may open up to someone else. What, you say that follow-up calls are not typical in your indus-

try? That's all the more reason to do it! Customers will be surprised to hear from you, and pleased that you care. Plus, it's good preventive maintenance.

Create Problem Solvers

I'm not referring to a nifty new product. By creating problem solvers, I mean empowering or enabling employees to solve problems for customers. Saturn's Customer Assistance Center once again comes to the rescue. In the last chapter, we covered how the center's first tier handles all the incoming mail and phone calls, up to the point of handling problem situations that can't be immediately resolved. Now we get to see how the problem solvers on the center's second tier handle the tougher situations.

You may recall that I explained (in Chapter 8) how the center's second tier consists of teams of customer assistance managers, who handle approximately 4,000 cases and 950 pieces of owner correspondence per month. There are four teams, each representing a region of the country: central, south, east, and west. There are 8 to 10 managers per team, and each manager handles 9 to 13 Saturn retail facilities. The managers play the very important role of liaison and help to facilitate solutions between the customer and the retail facility.

When further action is necessary at this level to resolve a problem, a case is opened. Actually, less than one-third of the calls received, and about one-fourth of the letters received, end up as cases. Let's say a manager has just opened a case on the customer problem of: "I have 50,000 miles on my car and the alternator just failed, and I think Saturn should pay to replace it." One manager now "owns" that case, meaning that he or she is responsible for the case from the beginning to the end of the resolution process. The customer is contacted, the situation is acknowledged, and levels of expectation are established. For example, resolving the problem "right away" may mean days or weeks to one person, or minutes or hours to another person, so timing is discussed. Then, thanks to technology, the manager has immediate access to all the warranty and service information on the car and alternator in question, which better prepares the manager to make decisions and suggestions. Detailed histories and notes are maintained on the case. The manager is empowered to do whatever it takes to resolve this customer's concern, which usually involves working hand-in-hand with the retailer in the customer's area. The case stays open until the problem is resolved. And the case is closed only after following-up with the customer.

Want to know what really makes Saturn's problem solving process work? Believe it or not, once again it comes down to this: *relationships.* Each manager has already worked to develop relationships with people at the retail facilities in the geographical area for which he or she is responsible. You see, the retailers are actually Saturn's first customers—as first purchaser of the cars. And you can't expect a retailer to take care of their customer if you're not supporting the retailer. So, each manager has a manageable number of retailers to work with, and develops those relationships through visits, getting to know the individuals on a first-name basis, and even with team-building exercises. Then, when the manager needs to contact the retailer to resolve a customer problem, the process is much smoother. The message here on developing relationships is similar to the title of Harvey Mackay's book on networking, *Dig Your Well Before You're Thirsty.* And while technology is an important part of the process, it does not begin to, nor will it ever, replace the importance of relationships.

That's not to say that only the folks in Saturn's Customer Assistance Center are problem solvers, and that there aren't other ways to solve problems. For example, when quality-related problems occur in the manufacturing process (which could ultimately create problems for customers), team members follow a step-by-step approach. The total quality problem-solving approach can be initiated by any team member. It involves assembling a crossfunctional team that seeks to pinpoint problems and identify solutions by methodically examining flowcharts of the job processes in the area where the problem occurred. After suggesting an interim fix, the team continues to analyze the problem, collect data, and develop a permanent solution. Then, its members attempt to validate their idea through a trial production run. Do you see similarities between this approach and the Customer Assistance Center's approach? There are several. They're both based on teams. They both have a defined process. They both empower team members to solve problems. They both follow the problem resolution process from beginning to end. And they both are effective at creating problem solvers.

WHAT YOU CAN DO

Create Problem Solvers

- Make it easy for people to feel empowered. If you're giving them responsibility, you must also give authority. For example, at an award-winning hotel, each housekeeper has the authority to spend up to $2,000 to solve a customer problem. The decision on when and how to spend the money is up to the individual housekeeper. A mission statement and values that are practiced can also help provide the comfort level and confidence needed for a person to feel capable as a problem solver.

- Let teams of employees work together to establish individual authority levels or to exchange ideas.

- Trust them to make the right decision.

- Teach them to be good listeners. Saturn's Customer Assistance Center Mission Statement refers to ". . . focus on understanding" and ". . . identifying opportunities." How can you do either if you're not focused on listening?

- Help them understand the positive consequences of problem solving. In other words, DO reward—DON'T punish.

- Don't set standards and goals based on the number of problems handled. Do focus on quality and problem resolution.

- Provide the information and technology that will help employees understand, monitor, and solve problems.

- Encourage employees to speak up and suggest solutions. Many times it is easier for them (rather than the boss) to see and fix problems with structure or procedure barriers within the company.

- Work on developing relationships between employees, suppliers, vendors, distributors, franchisees, or whoever should be part of the resolution process.

- Take action on employee input. Give employees feedback, whether the news is good, bad, or indifferent. They want to know what's going on! If employees get the impression that their input is going down a black hole, never to see the light of day, why should they continue to provide input?

- Freely give recognition for a job well done.

From Problems to Improvements

So now your customers are talking to you about their problems. Employees are providing input, and are busy preventing and solving problems. Is this all a waste of time that takes the company away from producing, selling, and making a profit? No, not if you learn from these experiences and use them as opportunities to improve.

A letter appeared in a Louisville newspaper's "consumer help" column a while back. A woman was complaining about her carpet cleaning experience. (Yes, the company was identified by name. This newspaper has a large readership base. In this case, an unhappy customer told a LOT more than 8 to 10 people about her unhappy experience!) Seems she hired this company to remove a stain, which it apparently did, and for which she paid "on the spot" (pardon the pun). However, as the day wore on, the spot began to get darker. The very next day, she called to complain. Four more times, on different dates, she called to complain. Still, nothing was done. She dutifully reported in her letter to the newspaper what she was told each time she called. On one of those calls, she even talked to the man who originally cleaned the spot.

Here's how the carpet cleaning company handled the situation. Management responded that it had no knowledge of the complaint until it received a letter from the newspaper columnist. Here's the kicker. The company president responded that "any one of our customers that phones our office concerning a problem with our work is told to phone me between 7 and 8:30 P.M. every Tuesday or Thursday . . . as that is when I personally take customer complaints."

WOW!—in the negative sense. The company president's response implies three things: (1) the customer is a liar, (2) the president doesn't trust his employees, and (3) the president doesn't want to be bothered with problems. I hope this situation served as a learning experience for that president and led to improvements, but I sincerely doubt it.

On the other hand, Saturn learns from problems and makes changes accordingly. First, lots of systems are in place to listen and learn of customer problems, and to capture and utilize the information learned. For instance, satellite communication links to the retailers allow service problems to be monitored in real time—to know customers' experiences as they happen.

Next, the information is shared, and is done so in a timely manner. The Customer Assistance Center is linked on-site to manufacturing, to immediately catch problems. Saturn's field organization is kept informed of customer issues through weekly and monthly reporting and trend information. When needed, Saturn's crossfunctional organization allows multiple disciplines to have input at team meetings and decide on changes.

Listening to customers has resulted in many product changes for Saturn, some small and some major. With early models, customers would get drenched when opening the car door after a rain. Calls poured into the Customer Assistance Center looking for a fix, which came via a major reengineering effort in 1996 and resulted in a world-class improvement. Other improvements resulting from problems or customer suggestions include incremental improvements each year to make the car quieter, a wider variety of car colors, and an adjustable-height shoulder strap (for which we shorter customers are thankful).

The voice of the customer is the heart of Saturn's product assessment process when it comes to changes or design. But, importantly, other voices are also heard and sought. Input comes from sales consultants, retailers, the customer and technical assistance centers, service and warranty records, surveys, research, and product clinics. A vehicle development team calls itself "the voice of the critical customer." Listen to the voices of all of your critical customers, from employees to vendors to end users. Then, take the next step to creating customer loyalty by converting criticism to improvements.

WHAT YOU CAN DO

From Problems to Improvements

- Have systems in place for capturing complaints and suggestions.

- Share the information with everyone involved in finding solutions.

- Have a cross section of people involved in making changes and finding solutions to major problems. No part of the company operates in a vacuum.

- Draw on a variety of information resources, both internally and externally.

- Use the information in a timely manner.

Turn Problems into Loyalty

Saturn had a real problem on its hands in October 1997. Faced with stiff competition, the company found it necessary to roll back prices on its 1998 models. Now remember, it's not the Saturn way to offer incentives or rebates. So what to do about the 14,000 customers who had already bought the new models? In a break from industry standards, Saturn very quickly sent refund checks to those customers, ranging from $300 to $960. Calls from unbelieving customers poured in to Saturn, asking "Is this check for real?"

Exceeding expectations is one way to turn problems into loyalty. It's kind of like the "baker's dozen," where you order and pay for twelve donuts but get thirteen. A good example of exceeding expectations when resolving a problem is found in Al's quote at the beginning of this chapter, about when he took his wife's Saturn in for some recall work. His expectations were exceeded when he picked up the car and found the gift of a $19.95 car-care kit inside, as a token for his troubles.

As customers, we generally want what is fair. We expect nothing less, or nothing more. That is why, many times, it doesn't take much to exceed expectations. Like one person going the extra mile, or a small token of appreciation, and the element of surprise. When delivering on these expectations, it will help to keep in mind the Golden Rules (from Chapter 6).

Follow up with a customer after the problem seems to be resolved, and you will not only exceed expectations, but you will help cement that loyal customer relationship. Why? Because most companies don't do it, so customers are surprised when it happens. Following up says "We care." Admittedly, following up can be a tough thing to do because it might be hard on our feelings and pride. We don't like to admit when we make mistakes or our products fail. We'd rather put the situation out-of-mind, and not have to confront the customer again. But, keep in mind that we are talking about building long-term relationships to create loyal customers. The old saying, "Love means never having to say you're sorry," doesn't apply here! Once sincere apologies are out of the way, the follow-up should focus on concern that the customer's needs are being met.

For example, there was an industrial supply company sales rep who convinced a customer to switch over to a new, different brand of pumps that were designed to work better than what the customer was currently using. Well, what actually happened was that the new pumps just didn't work as well as the older, less expensive pumps. The sales rep solved the problem by taking the new pumps back, but then he exceeded customer expectations by purchasing a supply of the original pumps and giving them to the customer—at no charge. On the follow-up visit, the rep was greeted by an ecstatic customer vowing continued sales orders with "just the type of vendor that we want to do business with."

Let's take a look at how Saturn works on turning problems into loyalty.

> *Back in the days of computer bulletin boards, I posted a question on Saturn's about a problem that my son had encountered when trying to purchase a Saturn. Not long after that, my son gets a phone call. I hear the typical teenager-style responses on my end, "Yeah, u-huh, okay." And finally, "Do you want to talk to my dad?" The guy on the other end was none other than the president of Saturn (Skip LeFauve). Unbelievable! He stayed on the phone until I ran out of questions; at least 15 minutes.*
>
> Al Clapsaddle

This next story is about problem solving when it's somebody else's problem. It comes from the owner of a van (definitely a non-Saturn product). Seems that over the weekend, her children accidentally let their two iguanas loose in the van. After capturing one, they assumed that the other one exited the van through an open door. The following Monday, the mother was driving to a job interview when she heard a scratching noise under the dashboard. She immediately exited the freeway and stopped at a nearby Saturn service department. A service representative—on his lunch hour—proceeded to remove part of the dashboard. He freed the iguana, safe and sound. Okay, so it wasn't a Saturn, and it wasn't the service technician's problem. But it was the right thing to do. And don't you think that whenever this woman or her family tells the iguana story, Saturn is named as the knight in shining armor? And don't you think that's good for business?

The Saturn sales consultant in this next story was awarded a "Moment of Truth Award" for his actions. I think the customer in this case was glad when her request for help was not met with the "It's not MY job" response. A gentlemen on his lunch break visited the Saturn showroom to look around, and explained that his fiancée had just put a deposit on a competitor's car. She loved the car, but neither of them liked the way they had been treated at "that other dealership." The Saturn sales consultant showed him around, and gave the guy a brochure and price list. About a week later, the man returned with his fiancée and she bought a Saturn. Now, it's important to realize that this story took place in the far Northeast, in the very, very cold month of February. Two weeks later, the Saturn sales consultant got a call from the man's fiancée. She had just locked her keys in her car. With the car running. With goldfish inside. Goldfish that were about to freeze. Solution? The sales consultant naturally took it upon himself to immediately take care of the problem. He personally made the trip, unlocked the car, and saved the goldfish. Later, some interesting things started to happen. The grateful customer wrote a thank-you letter. She started sending other people—with brochure and business card in hand—to her sales consultant. Fast forward . . . and the customer is married now. Perhaps a baby in the future? That's one way of creating customers for life!

Some Saturn customers have different kinds of problems: disabilities. These customers' cars may need some type of modifications or adaptive equipment, like wheelchair tie-downs, hand controls, or emergency-vehicle siren detectors. Since taking care of customers is the right thing to do, Saturn started a mobility program to help customers add adaptive equipment to their Saturns for barrier-free driving or riding. Teamwork, once again, is what makes this program work. Saturn works in partnerships with other folks to help the customers get the information they need to convert a Saturn to best meet their particular needs. These other folks include the customers' adaptive equipment installers, driver assessment centers, rehabilitation service providers, physicians, or physical therapists. Then,

Saturn exceeds expectations by helping pay for the equipment and installation, offering reimbursements of up to $1,000. To get started, customers can obtain a brochure on the program and a list of adaptive equipment installers in their area from their Saturn sales consultant, or by calling a toll-free number to the Saturn Assistance Center in Spring Hill. The brochure also provides helpful contact information on other related resources and associations. After the work is done, the customer completes an application form for reimbursement (provided by the Saturn retailer) and returns with the car to the retailer. The Saturn retailer confirms that the equipment has been installed, and the customer attaches a paid receipt for the work to the application form, and sends it off to Saturn. Four to six weeks later, the customer gets the check in the mail.

Here are two more stories that demonstrate how to exceed expectations:

> *I leased a Saturn and immediately moved to another state. There was a big hassle with transferring paperwork between the two states. Saturn has stood by me, and my salesman called me every day, almost three weeks after purchase, to help make sure I received my new state license plates. The temporary plate expired before I received my permanent license plate. My salesman made sure that Saturn paid for a rental car. He made numerous calls to my leasing bank, the department of motor vehicles, and to the state capitol to get things finalized.*
>
> Maria Hutzler

> *Within the first month, my automatic transmission got stuck in fourth gear and burned out. That made me think twice about the car I had just bought. But they came to my house and towed it in. The next morning, a limo came, picked me up, took me in to the shop to pick up a loaner. What service!*
>
> Lynn Huffman

WHAT YOU CAN DO

Turn Problems into Loyalty!
Exceed Expectations!

PROBLEM-SOLVING TIPS

KEY POINT

This key point comes in the form of a summary checklist for problem solving:

- Work toward preventing problems from developing in the first place.

- Listen to customers.

- Listen to employees and other people in-the-know.

- Create problem solvers by empowering employees.

- Respond promptly.

- Keep the customer informed during any resolution process.

- Capture information about problems; track resolution and results.

- Practice preventive maintenance by reviewing the services you provide after the sale.

- Use teams to find solutions to the big problems.

- Learn from problems and use them as opportunities to improve.

- Excel at turning problems into customer loyalty by exceeding expectations.

- Follow up with the customer after resolving the problem.

10

Keep Customers Coming Back!

"Will I See You Again?"

So what *really* keeps customers coming back to Saturn?

Well, there are lots of reasons. My car runs smoothly and without any problems. The service people are very friendly. They send postcards reminding me to change my oil. They send birthday cards for my car. They send newsletters. They get me in when I call for service, and don't give me a hard time.

Lynn Huffman

They hold road rallies, have customer appreciation days, and when you take your car in for service, they give you a bag of candy and wash your car for you.

Renee Minges

Aside from the fact that my car has been excellent, the people at the dealership are so nice, how could I NOT come back? (At the moment, I'm awaiting delivery of my second Saturn!)

Lynn Holberton

If the automobile's performance matches the sales and service performance I have thus far received, Saturn shall have me as a customer for life.

Henry B. Byrum Jr., M.D.,
a relatively new Saturn customer

Saturn is the best of all car dealerships. I have people ask me all the time if I really like my Saturn and if they are as good as everyone says—I say yes. I really love my Saturn. They really know how to treat their customers forever—not just for one day.

Linda Umbenhen

In 1993, I purchased a Saturn. I was very impressed with the friendly and "no pressure" way I was treated. I knew if I ever bought another car it would be a Saturn. I came back in August 1997 and purchased another Saturn.

Mary Chism

You can give customers lots of reasons to continue to do business with you. In fact, you *need* to give them lots of reasons to make them want to keep coming back. As you've already seen, customer loyalty is built on a combination of things resulting from the way you do business. And the true test of loyalty is when customers do come back and continue to buy your products and services.

Have you ever had customers apologize for not coming back? A small, family-owned pizza business used to send postcards to regular customers if they hadn't ordered for a month or so. The cards expressed concern, like "Where have you been? Have we done something wrong? If so, we'd like to apologize." Guess what happened. Customers actually called the company and apologized for not ordering pizza recently! (Then they'd make up for guilty feelings by ordering extra pizzas!)

Show Appreciation

Last summer, we got to take the whole family to Kings Island for Saturn's Customer Appreciation Day. I mean, there must have been about 15,000 Saturn owners there! The amusement park opened early just for us, and there was a picnic area set aside just for Saturn. Besides free lunch, there was music, and dancing, and activities for the kids. We got to see one of the new models. The only problem afterwards was trying to find MY Saturn in a sea of Saturns in the parking lot. Anyway, I don't know of any other car company that would do something like that. I guarantee that Saturn will continue to get my business!

Lynn Smith

Following up after the sale is like making the extra point after a touchdown in a football game and settling for a tie. However, showing appreciation is the equivalent of going for two points and winning the game. It's the icing on the cake, or the diamond anniversary ring.

Showing customers that you appreciate their business can be done in countless ways, ranging from simple thank-you notes to complex celebrations. Saturn's Homecoming event in 1994 is the model for the latter. Over a half-million invitations (see Exhibit 10.1) were mailed out, inviting owners to bring their car home to its birthplace—Spring Hill, Tennessee. And close to 44,000 enthusiastic people responded with an enthusiastic "Yes!" They stuck red balls on their cars' antenna, and joined up with caravans from all around the country. The two-day event was designed to provide something for every member of the family. In addition to the plant tours, there were plenty of other offerings:

- *Camp Saturn*—entertainment for kids ages 3 through 12
- *Saturn Excel Course*—fun team building activities for folks ages 13 through 18

Dear Saturn Owner,

By now, you may have heard rumors about something called "The Saturn Homecoming" coming up this summer. You may even have read about it in our newsletter, "Visions."

Well, it's all true, and it's all covered in the enclosed booklet. If you're wondering why we're holding such an event, the answer is this: we wanted to show our appreciation for the rather special relationship we have with our customers. And The Saturn Homecoming is the best way we could think of to give the people who drive our cars a chance to get to know the people who make and sell them--and vice versa.

So we hope you'll read this booklet and be able to come. If you can, please let us know as soon as possible--we think things are going to get pretty busy around here this summer. Just give us a call at 1-800-2-SATURN between 8:00 a.m. and 8:00 p.m. Central Time on a weekday (or between 9:00 a.m. and 3:00 p.m. on Saturday). The fee for the event will be $34.00 per adult and $17.00 for kids aged six to twelve (younger kids get in free). Once you've registered, you'll receive another mailing with more information, including a detailed schedule of events.

If, for some reason, you can't make it all the way to Tennessee, you might like to know that many retailers across the country will be organizing events of their own on that same weekend.

On behalf of the entire Saturn team, we hope that you'll join us. And thanks, once again, for being so supportive of our company and our cars.

Sincerely,

Skip LeFauve
President,
Saturn Corporation

John Michaud
UAW Advisor,
Sales, Service and Marketing

Exhibit 10.1   Saturn 1994 Homecoming Invitation

- *Team Town Expo*—a village full of folks who make Saturns, and over 80 different demonstrations, exhibits, and displays

- *Vintage Workshop*—featuring weavers, quilters, a blacksmith, and old-time storytellers

- *Antique & Custom Vehicle Show*—dozens of classics, roadsters, and a few rare sedans

- *Arts & Crafts Village*—more than a hundred local arts and crafts people showing and selling their wares

- *Entertainment*—music and more on three stages, plus roving entertainers

- *Food!*—fried chicken, roasted corn, cotton candy, and more, all reminiscent of old-time country fairs

- *Homecoming Concert*—with Wynonna Judd and BeBe and CeCe Winans, hosted by Olympic star Dan Jansen.

And although torrential downpours turned green fields to mud and collapsed a few of the big white tents, they didn't dampen spirits. I understand that even the potential problem of finding your car in a row of seven other medium-red SL2s was alleviated, by "Hello, my owner's name is ____" window stickers, supplied by Saturn.

This huge undertaking was possible due to the help of 2,000 volunteers—Saturn employees who worked on their own time to make it happen. Even though there was a cost to attend ($34 for adults, $17 for kids), the Homecoming was not—nor was it intended to be—a moneymaker for Saturn. It was a value for customers—with tickets included for one-day admission to nearby Opryland. Plus, part of the proceeds went to charity. Spreading the appreciation further, Saturn retailers around the country hosted regional events that summer for customers who couldn't make the trip to Spring Hill. They held barbeques, gave free car washes and oil changes, and collected donations for their charity partner. One retailer in New Jersey was able to donate $2,200 to Make-A-Wish Foundation.

By the end of the summer, more than 130,000 customers had been "appreciated," meaning that one of every six Saturn owners had participated in a Homecoming activity!

Think about this for a minute. Can't you just see a future of happy Homecoming survivors dragging friends and family to Saturn showrooms all over the country? Future purchases from loyal customers? Kids that were at the picnic returning in five or ten years to become Saturn owners themselves? Customers still talk about Homecoming '94 to this day, and dream of another one. When I attended a Saturn customer appreciation event in 1997, I spotted several customers wearing "I survived Homecoming 1994" T-shirts.

The event I attended in 1997 was a Saturn Customer Appreciation Day held at Paramount's Kings Island amusement park near Cincinnati (see Exhibit 10.2). This is the one that customer Lynn was referring to in her quote at the beginning of this section. It was a regional event, sponsored by 14 retailers in Ohio, Kentucky, and Indiana. It was pretty great. Saturn had a picnic area reserved and provided hot-dog lunches. There was music, dancing, and face painting, and several new models were on display, along with the Saturn Team race car. Even a little rain that day didn't wash smiles from faces of happy customers and their families.

Regarding a celebration on a little smaller scale, one man told me about the experience of his 81-year-old mother, a Saturn owner. She received a printed invitation from her local retailer to a chili dinner—in the showroom. After looking forward to it for weeks, she got all gussied up for that Friday night out. She enjoyed a hot bowl of chili, but admittedly was a little disappointed not to see her handsome young salesman there. Not to worry—her spirits were buoyed when some other fine Saturn gentleman asked her to dance. Well, for months afterwards, she

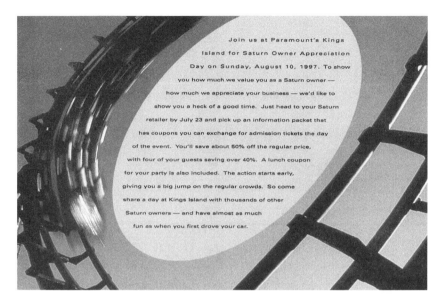

Join us at Paramount's Kings Island for Saturn Owner Appreciation Day on Sunday, August 10, 1997. To show you how much we value you as a Saturn owner — how much we appreciate your business — we'd like to show you a heck of a good time. Just head to your Saturn retailer by July 23 and pick up an information packet that has coupons you can exchange for admission tickets the day of the event. You'll save about 50% off the regular price, with four of your guests saving over 40%. A lunch coupon for your party is also included. The action starts early, giving you a big jump on the regular crowds. So come share a day at Kings Island with thousands of other Saturn owners — and have almost as much fun as when you first drove your car.

Exhibit 10.2 Invitation to 1997 Regional Customer Appreciation Day

went around telling all her friends about how "everybody at Saturn is so nice."

Why should *you* show customers that you appreciate their business?

First, because these loyal customers are keeping you in business. A small coffee service company had a major corporate customer in town that they had been doing business with for 10 years. To celebrate the anniversary and show appreciation, they gave a catered luncheon for the customer's entire staff (and it wasn't a small company!). The CEO explained his view this way: "The cost of the catered luncheon was actually small in comparison to the revenues that the customer represented to our company over a 10-year period."

Second, because showing appreciation is simply the right way to do business. Weren't you always taught to say "please" and "thank you"? Business relationships with loyal customers should be no different. Depending on the customer appreciation methods used, there are additional benefits to be realized:

- Exposing customers to other products or services that you have to offer
- Encouraging customers to spend more with you
- Encouraging positive word-of-mouth publicity
- Creating a great image
- Exceeding customer expectations
- Creating generations of customers

Now, before you get overwhelmed at the thought of a customer appreciation program for all of your hundreds, thousands, or millions of customers, let me offer a manageable solution. It doesn't *have* to be for ALL of your customers. In most businesses, there is what marketers call the "80/20 rule." It means that 20 percent of your customers account for 80 percent of your revenues. The point is that in your universe of customers, you generally have a small group of valuable, loyal customers. This is where you can begin your efforts. You do have a choice between all or none.

So, to show appreciation, you can host things like picnics and concerts, or outings to the amusement park, zoo, or sporting events. Just think of the variety of places to go and things to do. Or you can do something different and spend a lot less. I asked some other business people to share with me what they've done to show customer appreciation, and they did so enthusiastically and in great detail. But when I asked them what results they had seen or measured, the details were usually vague and not quantified. I heard responses ranging from "It was nice to see the smiles," to "I believe it will pay off in the long run in terms of repeat business," and "I just thought it was a nice thing to do." The ultimate true results are indeed often difficult to gauge, unless you view them in terms of customer loyalty. With that in mind, I will share "What Others Have Done" in the hope that it sparks ideas for "What You Can Do":

- In Louisville, Kentucky, home of the world-famous Kentucky Derby, a local uniform sales and service company takes advantage of that connection to show customer appreciation. Louisville is also home of the original, official, and delicious dessert-favorite Derby Pie.® Around Derby time, the two co-owners purchase and personally deliver about 150 pies to their customers. They explain that "you are such an important 'slice' of our success." They send an additional 20 to 25 pies to out-of-town customers. An added bonus may be a Derby Festival® lapel pin, "because we realize that successful businesses must 'pin' their future on their customers!" (Obviously, they're real punsters!) They try to deliver the pies at a time when they might actually catch customers in and see them. And when they do, some will say, "That reminds me; we need to place another order for uniforms." Other customers will take the time to write letters or call to say how much they enjoyed the pie. The company has been doing this for several years now, and as soon as Derby time starts to roll around again, customers begin hinting about how they're looking forward to getting their Derby Pie.®

- A real estate management company, whose customers include many homeowners or renters in the lower income brackets, delivers nice poinsettia plants at Christmas time. The company has received very nice thank-yous back from customers who say they have never received a poinsettia before, and some who have never had one for their home.

- A company that does pressure cleaning of decks and concrete surfaces sends thank-you letters to all customers. Upon completion of the job for their residential customers, they leave a potted plant or flower on their doorstep. The owner says it generates a lot of word-of-mouth referrals, and "100 percent customer satisfaction."

- For Valentine's Day, the owner of a home inspection service company personally delivers to her key customers bouquets of eye-catching bright red heart-shaped balloons. A balloon bouquet is different, and it celebrates a day not usually celebrated by businesses, yet the sentiment of building relationships is similar. An added bonus is that, since many of the company's customers are real estate and lending businesses, the balloons serve as an advertisement and generate the interest of potential customers.

- A retirement planning and investment company last year mailed profile request forms to about 300 clients, in which it asked them to list their hobbies, the date of their wedding anniversary, their favorite restaurant, their favorite author, and a past accomplishment or future goal. About 80 percent of the clients completed and returned their forms, giving the company great feedback. The information was entered into a custom-designed database (and the owners admit that they couldn't do a customer appreciation program without an automated system). Then they chose two vendors to start sending birthday gifts to clients. One vendor supplies and delivers steaks for the men; the other vendor handles dried floral arrangements for the women. After a year, they'll choose other gifts and vendors. They're also using the information now in their database to send personalized gifts for clients' wedding anniversaries, weddings, retirements, and other special occasions. The company owners chose this gift method of showing appreciation because it's like something a family member might do, and they want clients to consider them part of their family—especially since clients are trusting them with their financial future. The results thus far have been extremely positive. Tons of thank-you notes have poured in, and referrals have gone through the roof—with at least 100 good referrals. Then, when the company sends thank-you notes for referrals, it gets dozens of additional referrals!

- A photography studio celebrating 25 years in business sent select customers a letter of thanks, along with a gift certificate redeemable for $25 off their next photo session—plus a second certificate to pass along to a friend. Not only did the studio bring in $25,000 on this mailing (which cost less than $300 to produce in-house), it gained 16 new customers!

WHAT YOU CAN DO
Show Appreciation

- More formal customer loyalty programs, like VIP (Very Important Person, or Customer) and frequent buyer programs, can also be used to demonstrate customer appreciation and keep customers coming back. In order for programs of this nature to be successful, however, savvy homework is required. Things like identifying your most valuable and profitable customers, budgets, understanding and calculating value, commitment, and working out program details. Don't try to start a program of this magnitude without first tending to the details. I once received a letter from a store identifying me as one of their Very Important Customers, and offering me a great deal. Now, if I'm a very important customer of a store where I spent $20 on one visit two years previously, I have to wonder about the rest of their customers! Another example of missing the mark was a high-profile department store (whose name you would recognize if I mentioned it) that thought it had found a nice way to maintain customer loyalty. Seems the store sent special thank-you notes to big-ticket jewelry customers, who as it turned out were mostly men. Most of the notes were opened by women, the spouses of the gift-buyers. Unfortunately for the store, too many of these women had not been the recipients of the costly purchases. Whoops!

- Whatever way you decide to show customer appreciation, here are a few tips to consider:

  Be sincere, not gimmicky.

  Personalized or customized gifts for the recipient make an extra-nice touch.

  Just because you think your idea for showing appreciation is great doesn't mean that your customers will feel the same way. Find out if your efforts really are appreciated. One Saturn retailer inadvertently discovered how customers felt about its annual Christmas open house. The retailer would open the showroom on Sunday just for customers, serve hors d'oeuvres and hot chocolate, and pay admission for customers and their families to a major commercial lighting exhibit on the grounds next door. The fifth year of this event, invitations didn't get mailed to the entire customer list. Well, knowing the approximate date, a bunch of customers who were left off the list called the retailer, wondering why they didn't get an invitation. Not to worry; the retailer quickly corrected his error and sent invitations to the rest of the list. He also learned a lesson in customer appreciation!

- Just do it!

One Plus One Equals More than Two Customers

How do customers help other customers to keep coming back? They talk to each other. They share experiences. They compare notes. They spread the news—both good and bad. Chances are that with LOYAL customers, the good news will far outweigh the bad. You can help create the environment that will encourage customers to talk to each other.

I mentioned in Chapter 7 that many Saturn retail sales consultants were customers before becoming sales consultants. See, Saturn creates the treat-people-right environment that helps draw potential employees to them. And happy, loyal customers can make for happy, loyal, employees—and influence others to become Saturn customers. A Saturn service technician converted his father-in-law to Saturn cars—the same father-in-law who had 20-plus years of experience working for a competing car manufacturer.

On the Internet

Now for groups of customers that talk. Customers seem to put more stock in advice or information when it comes from "one of their own." (That's why word-of-mouth referrals work so great.) Customers can identify with other customers, since they are the ones who use the product or service. Some Saturn enthusiasts have created their own web sites, newsgroups, and e-mail groups, where they can swap stories, keep up on developments, and help each other with questions or problems. In my opinion, the premier web site is *Saturnalia,* the Saturn enthusiasts' site (see Exhibit 10.3). This is not an official Saturn site, nor is it sponsored or supported by Saturn in any way. It is designed, managed, and maintained by Charles Eickmeyer. You can check it out at: www.erols.com/core/—but be forewarned that sometimes the site moves around until a sponsor is found for a while. If that happens, just point your search engine to Saturnalia, and you shouldn't have any trouble finding it. Before I tell you about all the neat stuff on this site and how customers can talk to each other, let me first tell you about Charles.

Charles has no formal connection with Saturn Corporation. He's not even a customer! (However, he is waiting for the mid-size model and tells me he looks forward to purchasing a Saturn someday.) According to Charles, "I am just a fan who has made

The Saturn Authority for Saturn Enthusiasts

SATURN
Enthusiasts
Site

[Home l What's New l Interact l Library l Cars l Company l You l Links l FAQ l About l Send eMail]

Send your questions, comments, and suggestions to me at core@vt.edu.
- **What's New for June 8th**
- **Chat Every Thurs at 10pm**
- **Picture of the Week**
- **Future Saturns**
- **Saturn News**

1999 Preview

SATURN OWNER REGISTRY
Register You and Your Car

[Cars l Company l You]
[FAQ l About]

- **Question of the Week**
  If Saturn produces an SUV-like vehicle, what do you think it should be: a mini sport-utility or a modified SW2? Current responses.

- **Spy Photos Online**
  Catch a sneak peak at Saturn's upcoming LS sedan and wagon. Plus, see classic spy photos from Saturn's past. More to come! Read the S-Files.

- **Interactive Page**
  Exchange experiences. Express your feelings. Explore the ideas of other Saturn folks. Interact with other Saturn owners!

  "Sounds like they're worth $500." - *CINET* $69.99

LinkExchange Member

Exhibit 10.3   *Saturnalia*—Unofficial Saturn Web Site

a web site showcasing all of my ongoing research on the Saturn car, company, and owners. Following Saturn is a hobby of mine, and I enjoy volunteering my time to maintain the site." When does he find time to do that? Often it's late at night, when he should be sleeping.

Charles has been following Saturn since 1985. He was 10 years old when he first read about Saturn's "little red" prototype car. He was intrigued by the idea that an American car company could compete with the best from Japan. In high school and college, Charles often did projects which related Saturn to his classes. Sometimes the projects or papers were based on Saturn's unique union relationship, while others focused on its innovative engineering and branding techniques. Since Charles first started following Saturn, he's collected many articles, brochures, and accessories. He files all articles in 3-inch, 3-ring binders. Guess how many to date. Ten binders!

Charles created *Saturnalia* in the summer of 1996. It was a web site that focused on the latest Saturn news, reviews, and rumors. Charles wanted to create a place that would be a gateway for other enthusiasts to communicate with each other, and to connect them to the latest Saturn information on the Internet. The site was small, but grew quickly when he merged it with another Saturn enthusiasts' site (*Saturn Server*) in December 1996. To this day, Charles continues to maintain *Saturnalia* all by himself, and enjoys following the Saturn story. Why does he do it? In Charles' own words:

> My goal is to provide a place for Saturn owners and enthusiasts to interact and share their experiences, while helping potential owners discover how different Saturn really is. I've gotten quite a few e-mail messages from visitors who have said that *Saturnalia* convinced them to buy a Saturn. Many others have said it's the best Saturn site on the Internet—even better than the corporate site. That kind of feedback makes working on the site well worth all the time and effort.

And if that story doesn't impress you, his web site will. Most of the information comes from what Charles reads in magazines, newspapers, and various automotive news sites on the Internet. *Saturnalia* visitors also help keep the site current by sending Charles feedback. Here's what visitors to *Saturnalia* are likely to find:

- *What's New*—news items, usually updated weekly

- *Chat*—the opportunity to chat live on-line with other Saturn enthusiasts each Thursday night at 10:00 P.M.

- *Picture of the Week*—Saturn enthusiasts show off their cars

- *Future Saturns*—ideas from owners on what future Saturns should be, plus related news items

- *Saturn News*—current information or articles from magazines, newspapers, and various automotive news sources

- *Question of the Week*—just what it says, with the opportunity to post your answer and view what everybody else is answering

- *FAQ*—these Frequently Asked Questions and answers come from customers, based on their own Saturn car experiences

- *The Library*—the official resource room at *Saturnalia,* with links to automotive news resources, business news resources, magazines, automotive sites, car shopping resources, crash tests information, and traveling and weather sites

- *Cars/Company*—all about Saturn and the Saturn Differences, with links to the real, official Saturn Web Site

There's plenty more. "You" is where owners can send in their own Saturn stories and exchange experiences, link to other Saturn owners' home pages (one features a Saturn "geek code"), to Saturn CarClub sites, to the Enthusiasts Mailing List (e-mail), and to Saturn-related newsgroups.

Saturnalia is a popular site, getting around 5,000 hits each month. That number has been steadily increasing—it's up 150 percent over last year. Does Saturn Corporation tune in to see what all these loyal customers are saying? Charles says he has heard that the *Saturnalia* site is bookmarked on many computers in Spring Hill. Knowing how much Saturn values the voice of the customer, I'll just bet it is.

There you have it. Great opportunities for customers to talk to and help each other, and to help encourage each other's loyalty. And they really do, since these folks tend to be the real enthusiasts—about the car, the company, and about being a customer.

Through Customer Clubs

I'm a CarClub member. I like what they stand for. They do charitable things and honestly enjoy helping others. They're real people.

Patricia Clum

Sometime in the early 1990s, Saturn customers started to get together and form clubs. Today, there are over 160 CarClub chapters around the country. The CarClubs, whose logo is a heart on wheels, are all about having fun, meeting new friends, and helping out in the community. The CarClub's "Pledge of Honor" says it all, (see Exhibit 10.4).

Many clubs have their own custom-written mission statements which emphasize societal goals as much as social ones. Some CarClub chapters have their own Internet sites or newsletters. Saturn has supported the clubs' growth by providing guidance on how to start a chapter; providing literature, banners, and newsletters; and by processing national membership applications and dues. Local Saturn retailers, referred to as "Champions," play the key role of assisting their CarClub chap-

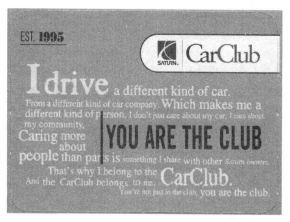

Exhibit 10.4   Saturn CarClub Pledge of Honor

ters, including helping with events, providing meeting places, and sometimes hosting the club's web site. However, this is a club where members aren't just in the club, they *are* the club.

New Saturn owners are beckoned to join the club in various ways: by other members, through brochures with enrollment forms available at retail facilities and at events, and through information on Saturn's web site. When I attended the New Owners Clinic, we were told about the club, and brochure enrollment forms were included in information packets that we received. When I joined at the Membership Plus level (a national enrollment fee of $25 at that time), I received a membership card, a CarClub window decal, a minicatalog of CarClub stuff available for purchase through the retailer, a subscription to the member-to-member quarterly newsletter (the *Connector*), a preregistered key tag (if keys are lost, the finder merely drops them in the mail and they get returned to the owner), a glove-box road atlas, and the all important CarClub T-shirt. (Appropriately, the back of the shirt reads, "If you don't own one, you probably wouldn't understand.") The Car-

Clubs are continuing to evolve—more so at the local level—and when I renew my membership in the future, I'll simply need to pay chapter dues, with no national enrollment fee.

Back in Chapter 8, I mentioned the CarClub newsletter, the *Connector*. That's where many of the clubs' activities and good deeds are shared. The following list will give you an idea of some of those activities and good deeds, then I'll share a few details with you.

Some Saturn CarClub activities:

- Car washes that send kids to camp
- Picnics that help build parks
- Barbecues at nursing homes
- Food drives
- Canoeing and biking outings
- Clean-a-highway programs
- Pool parties
- Road rallies
- Senior home visits and sharing homemade goodies
- Fund-raisers and benefits for charity
- Bingo and card games
- Progressive dinners
- Toys for children at Christmas
- Pilgrimages (visits) to Spring Hill
- Scavenger hunts
- Playground-building projects
- Trips to neat and famous places
- Easter baskets for women's shelters

- Holding-pen project for injured wildlife at sanctuary
- Food to the Humane society
- Garage sale fund-raiser
- School supplies to crisis center
- Staff booth at car shows
- Selling boards for use in building a Habitat for Humanity home
- Collecting bikes for a recycle program
- Thanksgiving dinners to needy
- Fun run/walk for charity
- Informational meetings
- Chili cook-off
- Service miniclinics
- Collecting items for Ronald McDonald House
- One-week cruise to Cozumel and Grand Caymen Islands!

Pretty extensive list, huh? Now here are a few details. The Fort Worth CarClub participated in its city's annual Parade of Lights at Christmastime, entering nine Saturns in the parade, one for each of Santa's reindeer. Each car was bedecked with lights, a sign bearing its reindeer name, and large wooden antlers. Of course, Rudolph had a red nose light!

The Route 66 CarClub of Springfield, Missouri, read an article about a woman who runs a shelter for animals rescued from abusive homes. She was holding down three jobs just so she could afford the more than $2,000 in monthly veterinary bills. The CarClub decided to do its share by washing cars for donations. Thanks to contributions from the community and extra help from the retailer, the CarClub successfully raised both money and awareness for their cause.

The Gateway Chapter of St. Louis supported the Give-a-Meal-a-Month program, with members donating a specific list of groceries that needy families could then use to prepare an entire dinner from start to finish.

Selling lumber to passing motorists? That's what the Planet White Plains (New York) CarClub did. It was all part of the club's fund-raiser on behalf of Habitat for Humanity. For a $10 donation, drivers "bought" a 2 × 6 board, which was then used to help build a home for a local family.

That's just a sampling, folks. I could probably fill an entire book with all the CarClub stories. Members talk to each other, help each other, help the community, have fun, and seem to enjoy eating (food being somewhat of a common denominator during the fun activities and meetings).

WHAT YOU CAN DO

On the Internet and through Customer Clubs

Consider supporting your loyal customers through a web site. Options include:

- Hosting or advertising on their site
- Providing links on your own site to theirs
- Sharing their stories on your site
- Giving them means to talk with each other through your site

Is a club of some type right for your business? Clubs formed for customers around a common interest are useful for keeping customers coming back. A bookstore, for example, might form a "mystery readers club." A plant nursery could have a "perennial growers club." Members benefit from the company's expertise, and are rewarded with special benefits or discounts. Businesses are rewarded with loyal customers that keep coming back and spending more.

Look over the list of Saturn CarClub activities—not only for ideas that you can use in your business to keep customers coming back—but also for ideas on how to:

- Get customers talking to other customers
- Help employees meet customers
- Show customer appreciation
- Get involved in the community
- Reinforce the business' basic values

Keep Listening to Customers

Keep customers coming back by continuing to listen to them. Businesses get into trouble and lose loyal customers when they start assuming that they know what's best for customers. The first step in Saturn's "Six Steps To Customer Enthusiasm" begins with "LISTEN to your customers . . . don't assume," and you've seen evidence throughout this book of Saturn doing just that. One more way that Saturn incorporates the voice of the customer is through the use of focus groups.

The basic idea behind focus groups is to put 15 or 20 people (in this case, your existing customers) in a room and give them food and a few bucks in exchange for their opinions on your products or services. Focus groups can be assembled and conducted by the company or with the help of a facilitator (an impartial, outside observer who won't bias the results). More commonly, they are handled completely by market research firms. For a price (starting at around $2,500), an outside firm will line up participants, refine questions, and provide a neutral moderator.

Saturn mixes it up, depending on the situation—doing its own focus groups, using outside firms, and sometimes doing its own design but using an outside firm to conduct the groups. They utilize focus groups on various subjects, from product changes to direct mail. For instance, some results of focus groups say:

- Most owners open all mail from Saturn.
- All that mail is almost expected, based on the sales experience.
- Owners trust the Saturn retailer for service, based on the sales experience.
- Owners think the retailer knows their Saturn best.

Saturn did a series of a focus groups all over the country to get ideas on what customers want and like, along the lines of "What can we do in the retail process to make customer experiences more pleasurable?" For this series, however, they invited more than just Saturn customers. Also invited were sales consultants, target market buyers, customers of their competition, and people from companies outside the industry but known for excellent customer service—like Nordstrom. Saturn would take the ideas, boil them down into a smaller set, then have customers sort them out in order of importance. It was then up to Saturn to make the best of the focus groups' results, and to determine exactly what it could do. And that is just another way that Saturn continues to listen, in order to keep customers coming back.

I mentioned earlier the danger of assuming, such as the "I've been doing this for 25 years and I know my customer" approach. The vice president of a chain of formal-wear rentals and sales stores thought he knew what customers wanted in terms of new tuxedos for prom rentals. But he went ahead and spent about $1,000 to do his own focus group. He presented *his* top three picks to the group. Boy, was he surprised when the focus group shot down all three! The group then helped him "focus" on styles and marketing strategies that they found attractive, and saved the VP from investing $60,000 on ineffectual products and strategies. He also learned an important lesson about keeping customers.

WHAT YOU CAN DO
Keep Listening to Customers

- Besides creating focus groups to continue listening to your customers, another way to listen is through an advisory team or council. Many companies that franchise or manufacture have something like an "advisory council," either formally or informally. Their franchisees or distributors are the company's first customers. So the company invites these customers to have a voice by serving on an advisory council. Saturn's advisory council has a little different twist. It's really the Franchise Operations Team (FOT), a joint team between Saturn and its retailers. The franchise agreement requires that this team make all the decisions—in the consensus decision-making style—as to how the distribution system is run. (Usually, with an advisory council, advice is sought from the members, but the company makes the decisions and doesn't even have to take their advice.)

- You can create your own informal customer advisory council. Select and personally invite some of your most valuable customers to "partner" with you on this council, and you both will benefit. Schedule a meeting once or twice a year. An agenda is a must. It's also important that customers can speak openly, without fear of hurt feelings or breach of confidential information. Share the company's plans and concerns. Ask these "customers in the know" to help you, so that you can better help them. "What features of our widget are most important to you? What features would you change? How could we make it easier to use? How much do you value these related services that we provide?" Then listen and learn from their advice, and take notes. Don't forget to thank your customer partners. Reward them with recreational activities, dinner, entertainment, or free products or services. These loyal customers now share a somewhat vested interest in the company. A manufacturer of industrial products recently took this approach to help launch a new product line. It invited current and potential distributors and some end users to town for a product meeting, plant tour, and some entertainment. That's just one more way to continue to listen to and learn from your customers.

Keep Track of Customer Information

My wife and I bought a new Saturn in 1993. Several years later when our daughter needed a car, we looked at buying a used Saturn that an individual had for sale. Even though it wasn't through a Saturn dealership, I called the Saturn plant and asked for the maintenance history on the car. And they had it! It's really great that you can get a printout of the service history.

Randall Griggs

The path to keeping customers coming back is more easily navigated if customer information stays on track. Think about what's involved with keeping up with your best friend. You note your friend's birthday on your calendar. You record your next get-together in your planner. You have the address and phone number written down somewhere, maybe in several places. Four previous addresses are scratched out, because you keep track of your friend's moves. You know your friend's likes and dislikes, and what present you gave on his or her last birthday. Your friend gets married and has children. You know the spouse's name, and the kids' names, ages, and interests. Maybe you keep that information in your memory. Now imagine trying to keep up with a million friends in the same manner. In the business world, we rely on computers to help us manage all this information. It's a big job—with a big payoff—if the information is managed and used properly.

Thanks to technology, if while traveling I need to take my car in for service to a Saturn retailer on the other side of the country, the retailer can very quickly access my previous service records. This saves me from having to jog my memory for details (which will likely be inaccurate) and repeat them to a stranger. Like a friend, Saturn remembers and keeps track of our encounters. Although I guess that could have the possibility of telling on me—as was the case illustrated in a recent Saturn commercial. A guy driving his Saturn across the country keeps stopping at Saturn service departments to report minor problems. As the technician at each of these facilities checks out the supposed problem, the customer avails himself of the free doughnuts in the waiting area. The technician doesn't find any problem, and sends the customer on his way. After about the fifth stop at yet another Saturn retailer, we see the service writer scanning his computer screen, which shows the previous stops and service records—all indicating that no problem was found. But wait . . . there it is, at the bottom of the screen: "LIKES JELLY DOUGHNUTS."

As is common in the automotive industry, vehicles are tracked by their vehicle identification number (VIN). Not so common is how Saturn manages that information—with the help of GM's

Electronic Data Systems (EDS—Ross Perot's old company) and satellite communication systems linking retail facilities. This type of system enables entries and changes to be made quickly, with single entry. What all this means to me as a customer is that it's seemingly effortless for Saturn to keep track of my car, and of me as long as I'm the owner. For instance, when I take my car in for service, by entering my VIN into their computer, the service associates quickly have my name, address, phone number, and service history of my car. If my address has changed, I only have to tell them once. By entering the new address—right there in the service department computer—all my records throughout Saturn are updated. If correspondence is mailed in the future, whether it's from my retailer, Spring Hill, or elsewhere in Saturn Corporation, it will come to my new address.

Not that Saturn has to rely on me to visit my retailer in order to update information. Mailings requesting that I update my records help, and one I received doubled as a satisfaction survey (see Exhibit 10.5). Just more evidence of how Saturn is continuing to listen to customers.

Retailers can choose to handle customer correspondence themselves, or may use the services of Saturn Customer Communications (SCC). In fact, SCC came about as the result of a primary decision on the part of Saturn and their retail partners to strengthen the entire Saturn ownership experience through a two-way communication process. As mentioned in Chapter 8, things like welcome letters, birthday cards, maintenance reminders, thank-you cards, and newsletters can be coordinated, customized, and mailed under this program. The mailing list database can be maintained and updated for the retailer by SCC.

On an individual level, sales consultants at Saturn retail facilities are apt to use different systems to keep up with their customers and maintain personal information, including card systems or even the old-fashioned paper files method. I find that true of salespeople in general. Seasoned salespeople each

SATURN OF LOUISVILLE

#2 Swope Auto Center
Louisville, KY 40299
Phone:(502) 499–3800

SATURN.

All of us at Saturn recognize that things change. Which is why we like to go through our records once in a while and make sure that they, at least, are up–to–date. And you can help us a lot by taking the time to answer a few questions. Not only would it ensure our records are accurate, it would let us know how you think we are doing.

Our records show:

Owner Name: **Phone:**
Address: **Delivery Date:**
                                                               VIN:
                                                               Model:

COMPLETE ONLY IF DIFFERENT FROM ABOVE

Name _____
                    (First)   (M.I.)   (Last)

Address _____
                    (Number & Street)   (City)   (State)   (Zip)

Phone Number_____ E–mail_____
                    (Area Code)   (Phone Number)

1) Do you still own this Saturn?   ☐ Yes   ☐ No

   If your Saturn has been sold, please indicate that person's name, address and phone number below:

Name _____
                    (First)   (M.I.)   (Last)

Address _____
                    (Number & Street)   (City)   (State)   (Zip)

Phone Number_____ E–mail_____
                    (Area Code)   (Phone Number)

2) Please check, if applicable: ☐ This Saturn is no longer in service.

3) What is the current mileage on your Saturn?_____ miles as of ___ /___ /___

4) Everything we learned about customer satisfaction we learned from Saturn owners like you. So, please give us your honest opinion. Please check the box which best reflects how you feel about:

	COMPLETELY SATISFIED	SATISFIED	NEITHER	DISSATISFIED	COMPLETELY DISSATISFIED
a) Your new Saturn	☐	☐	☐	☐	☐
b) Your Saturn sales consultant	☐	☐	☐	☐	☐
c) Your Saturn delivery experience	☐	☐	☐	☐	☐
d) The way we handled your financial arrangements	☐	☐	☐	☐	☐

5) What can we do better? _____

6) You've probably heard about the Saturn CarClub, a way for Saturn owners to get together. If you haven't joined already, and you'd like more information, please check here: ☐

If you have any additional comments about us, your Saturn, or anything else, please let us know below:

_____

_____

_____

Thanks for your help. When completed, please fold, seal, and drop into any mailbox.

Exhibit 10.5   Saturn of Louisville Customer Update Form

have their own system that works for them, electronic or otherwise. If it works effectively for customers, and if it works for the company, that's all that matters. Saturn does offer sales consultants the tools and the know-how to effectively follow up. In a half-day seminar, participants receive a simple card file system designed to record, track, and prompt customer contacts. The system is designed to be flexible, can be easily customized, and can be used as a stand-alone system or integrated with in-facility computerized follow-up systems.

Why bother to keep track of all this information? Ideally, because it will pay off in terms of customer loyalty. Maintaining and properly managing customer information can help you do the following:

- Keep in touch with customers on a consistent basis

- Know customer needs (like the fact that a good customer's son turns 16 next month and will be needing a car)

- Make it easier to show customers that you care

- Know what product or service changes or improvements need to be made

- Know who your best customers are, and know which customers have the potential to move into the best customer category

- Cross-sell (i.e., sell additional products or services), and do so more easily

- Measure, track, and test results

- Keep customers coming back!

And if computerized customer information management systems are used, there's another advantage—the ability to customize and print out all types of reports that can help with strategic planning and decision making. Reports like these:

- Key accounts not visited in the last 30 days
- Sales history by customer
- Customer purchasing by segment or product
- Most valuable customers
- Customer sources (i.e., referrals, etc.)

I've seen many companies (and even used to work for a few of them) where the keeper of customer information was the accounting department. The fine folks in accounting could tell you anything you wanted to know about customer numbers. But if you wanted to know the real customer relationship stuff, you were out of luck—especially if the salesperson who had all the stuff in his or her head left the company. Fortunately, all of that is changing now. Technology makes it possible to merge the numbers with the rest of the customer information. And we're getting smarter about managing that information to help build long-term customer relationships.

WHAT YOU CAN DO

Keep Track of Customer Information

Take an investigative look at all the areas where various forms of "customer intelligence" are lurking in your business. Chances are you'll find bits and pieces scattered about in the following locations:

- Filing cabinets
- Point-of-sale records
- Sales reps call reports
- Mailing lists
- Billing records
- Engineering

- Order processing
- Service records

That's okay. You want and need this information. In fact, the more information you have about each one of your customers, the easier it is to keep them coming back. The trick is in coordinating the information. And the danger is in the right hand not knowing what the left hand is doing.

Let's say that you are a salesperson for 10 different models of widgets, and you're getting ready to call on an existing customer. In order to meet that customer's needs and to keep that customer, what would be helpful to know before making that sales call?

- The current contact person, and that person's interests
- Which widgets were purchased last
- When they were purchased
- How many widgets were purchased last year
- Notes from your last conversation with the customer about their plans for expansion (i.e., the need for more widgets)
- The manner in which the customer prefers to order, and previously arranged payment terms
- Any recent service problems on the last shipment of widgets

Now, what you don't want to happen when you meet with the customer is to hear (from the customer) that they just received notice from your company's accounting department that their account has been placed on C.O.D. (News to you!) And they just received a mailing from your company about potential problems with the widgets they last ordered. (Again, news to you.) Or that they just tried to place an order for 1,000 widgets, but one of your engineers told them that the modifications they requested could not be done. Period. (Surprise—you know it's been done before.)

That's a lot of information to keep up with, and a high potential for communications with the customer to get mixed up. Fortunately, there are many affordable, off-the-shelf customer management software programs on the market now (like Gold-Mine and Act!) to help you manage. Some systems allow you import or export data so that you can combine customer contact information with accounting information. There are also ways to manage and coordinate the information internally, so that the right hand *does* know what the left hand is doing. The point is that you must have a coordinated effort to keep in touch with customers, to project a consistent image, and to keep customers coming back.

Plan for Future Growth

If you're keeping in touch, listening, and learning from customers, that will make it easier for you to plan your company's future growth. At Saturn's Homecoming, they had new car models on display with product information booths. And, to plan for the future, they also had booths set up to listen and gather suggestions about how to improve the car. Saturn continues to listen, and plans to "grow with their family" by introducing a midsize sedan in 1999 and possibly a sports utility vehicle in 2001. Plus, EV1—the GM electric car—is already available through Saturn retail facilities in California and Arizona.

In a real turnabout (although it took ten years), Saturn began selling cars in Japan in 1997. Remember, the Japanese small car imports were the driving force in the birth of Saturn. Of course, Saturn did its homework and made some changes based on customer needs and wants. (Interestingly, the most popular car models in Japan are wagons.) One thing that won't change is Saturn's straightforward sales approach and "no-hassle, no-haggle" way of doing business. See, in Japan, when you're ready to buy a car, the retailer brings a car to your house and may even stay for dinner. Since Saturn has always gone the extra mile for customers, they'll fit right in. One thing that does change in Japan is the tag line. Instead of "a different kind of company," a revised tag line means (translated) "the company and car with the deepest respect for people." It's all about treating people right.

What a lot of Saturn customers find nice is the ability to customer-order vehicles. One of Saturn's competitors recently admitted their big problem is that customers often wait weeks for delivery, and then they must accept cars with options they don't want. A spokesperson said, "We have to figure out how to give customers the car they want, when they want it, and how they want it."[9] Yep, that will help to keep customers coming back!

KEEP THE WHEEL TURNING

Remember to say thanks to your customers for keeping you in business. Find ways to show appreciation. Encourage customers to talk to and help each other. Keep listening to customers, individually and through groups or councils. Use technology to maintain, manage, and utilize customer information. Analyze and meet future needs. Find ways to customize.

Remember that customer loyalty is not the result of any one thing. It's built on a combination of things resulting from the way you do business. The "wheel" model for customer loyalty (Chapter 3) starts with treating people right, and turns to produce loyal customers and increased profitability. So, start your engine, and keep that wheel turning!

The Rest of
The Story

ᴄᴴᴬᴾᵀᴱᴿ
11

Q's & A's
with a Saturn Big Wheel

OKAY, READERS, SINCE I'M NOT A SATURN INSIDER, I FIGURE THAT some of you may have questions and would like answers from somebody at Saturn who is actually "at the top and in the know." Since I couldn't talk to each of you individually before this book was published, I did the next best thing. I formed a small review committee consisting of a cross section of business people from manufacturing, product, service, and distribution companies, who represented industrial, commercial, and retail firms. After they read an early draft of this book, I challenged the group with this question: "If you could sit down with the leaders of Saturn and ask them questions related to customer loyalty, what would you ask?"

Joe Kennedy, Saturn's vice president of sales, service and marketing, graciously agreed to an interview. So, to satisfy anticipated curiosity, here is your question and answer forum.[10]

Question: How do you feel that customer loyalty has contributed to Saturn's success?

Answer: Let me start by saying that you actually hear the words *customer loyalty* very, very rarely around Saturn. As you know, we much more frequently talk about the term *customer enthusiasm.* The only reason I mention that is because loyalty is an outcome. If you ask people about our goal, I think most people would say our goal is customer enthusiasm, and clearly that results in customer loyalty. So, how has it contributed? Clearly, in two ways:

1. We have now been around long enough that there is loyalty in the repurchase sense of the word, and we have a terrific repurchase rate—especially for a company with such a limited product line. The data on the industry says that for people who purchase a car in one of our segments—small & sporty—the general migration pattern in our industry is for half of those people to make their next purchase outside of small & sporty. Our indication thus far is that, for the half that repurchase in small & sporty, we are getting virtually all of them. I don't have the specific statistics off the top of my head, but based on the first stat that the universe for potential repurchase loyalty is 50 percent of our total owners, I think we're getting like 47 percent of the 50 percent. But that is repurchase loyalty, and we view that as just one component—maybe not even the most important component of customer enthusiasm.

2. We strongly believe that—as much as we, like other auto marketers, spend money on advertising and other things—at the end of the day, cars is a word-of-mouth business. The car that you buy is more shaped by the word-of-mouth opinion you receive from family, friends and coworkers than it is shaped by any other method. And we believe the enthusiasm that we have generated amongst our customers has generated positive word of mouth to an extraordinary extent, and *that,* more than anything else, has fueled our sales success. Even by our standards, last year was not

great, yet we were still the fourth-best-selling car to retail customers in the entire country.

I would say about how it has contributed to our success: The word of mouth, as well as the repurchase loyalty, are pure indicators of customer enthusiasm.

Question: Did Saturn start with the objective of creating customer loyalty, or did small actions snowball?

Answer: I distinctly remember back when Don Hudler (Saturn's current president) came on board in 1987. I had actually been on for almost two years before he came on board, in the vice president, sales and marketing position. Don very clearly and consistently started talking about customer enthusiasm. And to be honest, it was not a term most—if any of us—had ever heard before. To tell you the real story, I think I and some others walked around probably for months, not knowing exactly what the guy was talking about. But through repetition, and through building on, it became kind of a specific project. There was a lot of analysis of the whole "moments of truth" kind of concept. This is a long-winded way of saying that where we ended up was not an accident. I tend to think much of the strategy in business evolves and you stumble on things. You question if small actions snowball, and obviously that makes sense. I think from 1987 on, starting with Don, customer enthusiasm became a mantra and we got more and more behind it in terms of substance that made it real. By the time we showed up for market in 1990, the strategy was pretty well developed and comprehensive, and pretty thoughtful (as opposed to kind of stumbling into it).

Question: Some of the things that Saturn and their retailers do sound too good to be true. What steps does Saturn take to help prospective buyers believe that it is all for real?

Answer: That's a great question, and we kind of struggle with it. We do systematically collect stories and review them for advertising decisions—our advertising is overwhelmingly true customer stories. We have on numerous occasions rejected stories for advertising because of our fear that people would not believe them—that they were literally too good to be true. We actually just did that on a story that we had developed with the ad agency about someone who returned a car using the Saturn money-back guarantee. The story was of a graduate who bought the car, and her teenage brother borrowed it without her permission. He trashed it drinking beer with his buddies. She was appalled that her new car had been trashed, so she money-backed it and we gave her another car. But that's one of those things that people wouldn't believe.

My best answer to this question is that really, it's a word-of-mouth business. Whatever we say really is much less important than what people say to each other. We view word of mouth as our primary advertising mechanism, and the great thing about word of mouth is that it's entirely credible. What steps do we take? Above and beyond everything else, we stick to the truth when we tell stories in advertising and other mechanisms. If anything, we try to pick stories that are credible and are representative of what people can realistically expect to experience.

Question: Car buyers have been conditioned since the beginning to expect to bargain, or a "deal." How does Saturn overcome this built-in tendency by the customer to want a bargain?

Answer: The first thing I've observed is that it was a lot harder early on than it is now. Now that we've got a solid reputation, people kind of understand we're the no-haggle, no-hassle folks. I have to smile when I tell you this. Occasionally I hear a story that some negotiating-oriented buyer comes to a Saturn retail facility and takes a want ad, cut-me-a-deal kind of approach. When the sales consultant indicates that at Saturn we don't hassle or haggle, that we believe in a true value for our cars up-front, those people occasionally will say "Yeah, yeah, I know that, but I wanted to test you and see if it was really true." So even those oriented towards negotiation, I think at this point have learned. Much earlier on, I think it really took a great deal of training and buy-in to what we were doing, for the sales consultants and the retailers to understand the value of no-hassle and no-haggle as part of our culture.

The single most important thing, beyond training and culture, is how we approach pricing. When we figure out the MSRP (manufacturer's suggested retail price) of a Saturn, we don't compare our MSRPs with the MSRPs of other competitors. What we do is we take their MSRPs, and we gather a lot of data through a variety of sources on how much their dealers discount. We look at how much haggling will actually get you at a Toyota store or Honda store or whatever. Then we also take into account what kind of incentives, rebates, etc., that Honda, Toyota, etc. run. We knock that all down and compute the honest-to-God real prices at which our competitors transact after two hours of negotiation at a Toyota store (what's a Corolla really going to cost you?), after two hours of haggling at a Honda store (what's a Civic really going to cost you?), and we estimate that. It's no small amount of effort we put into the process. Then we price our vehicles to be a value versus that price. Our MSRPs are set to be a value versus what we call the transaction price of our competition. That discipline by us from a pricing standpoint in essence guarantees that: we at Saturn provide you the customer with a better price up front, and with no-hassle no-haggle, than you can get after two hours of hassle and haggle at our competitors. So that approach to pricing, along with a great deal of cultural development and training in terms of retail selling, is really how we built that reputation from the beginning and how we continue it today. It's how we priced our cars in 1990, and that pricing approach is still how we go at it today.

Question: How much of the way that Saturn people treat customers is training, and how much is natural?

Answer: I would slightly rephrase the question to "How much of it is training processes, and how much of it is cultural?" I strongly believe that companies that deliver great service always have some combination of great systems and processes, or a great customer-oriented culture. Think about Southwest Airlines or Disney, or others. Disney, I think, is an example. Disney thinks through everything. What looks so natural at Disney takes processes and processes and processes. They think about how a ticket should be taken, and they teach people the process to take a ticket, punch a ticket, give a ticket back, make eye contact, smile. It's very heavy on systems and processes. Southwest Airlines, I think, is much less that way—it's much more cultural phenomenon and customer orientation.

Most of the great stories you hear about customer experiences at Saturn are not things that we specifically ever trained people to do. We give people training; we do a tremendous amount of training. But one of the observations about service situations—particularly automotive shopping and service situations—is that so many situations can arise. Quite honestly, it's incredibly daunting to try to imagine every single situation and train someone how to handle it. So, our approach tends to be a pretty serious in-depth training approach in basic customer processes. We teach people a process for selling, and we teach people a process for service consultation, but our training is unique in that it is loaded with cultural training. And the value of establishing a very strong culture that's built on some clear values and a philosophy is in all of those customer situations where you haven't provided true training on a specific answer. The culture, the values and philosophy will guide the person on the front line to the right answer instinctively.

I would describe us as one part systems and processes, and three parts culture, values, and philosophy.

Question: What are the difficulties that Saturn faced—and continues to face—in running a company with such a distinct culture as compared to the rest of General Motors?

Answer: Honestly, this is not a particularly big issue that's on my mind. We have had an extraordinary amount of independence from GM from day one; we actually are working more with GM now than before. But GM has a lot of respect for Saturn's cultural difference and tries pretty hard not to mess with it.

A more interesting question would be, "How did ever such a distinct culture get developed in the first place?" At its current point, it's so well developed and so well respected that I think GM (as I said) tries pretty hard not to mess with it. The work of the 99 [see Chapter 2]—that's kind of an extraordinary story in corporate history, where a group would be sanctioned to go off and think the way they were sanctioned to go off and rethink the business. And then I think quite honestly that Skip [Skip LeFauve, Saturn president 1986–1994] is just an absolutely extraordinary leader, and that culture developed as well as it did in large part because Skip shepherded it. Very few people have ever shepherded a culture as rooted in values and philosophy.

Question: How has the successful part of the Saturn philosophy been transferred to the rest of General Motors, and why hasn't the entire philosophy been adopted by the rest of the GM organization?

Answer: My reaction to this is that cultural advantages tend to be extremely hard to duplicate, because cultures tend to arise through the history of organizations and the history of leaders that they have. When people ask me various versions of this question, I say it's kind of good news and bad news. The bad news is GM just can't pick up and do what we did and duplicate it. The good news is what Saturn has done is truly a sustainable competitive advantage. Quite honestly, if GM could have just picked up what we did and duplicated it, well, I wouldn't be able to explain why Toyota and Honda and everybody else couldn't pick up what we had done and duplicate it. I think that goes back to the extraordinary difficulty of developing our culture and nurturing it, and once a strong culture has been developed it's extremely hard to duplicate. That said, I think GM and many different parts of GM have picked up a great deal from Saturn, but it is difficult to duplicate our culture.

Saturn, more so than most success stories—if you want to call us a success story—is very "holistic." I generally don't like that term, but in Saturn's case it applies. Having been here a long time, I've watched all sorts of people from all sorts of organizations (and this goes far beyond GM) come to Saturn and try to pick up the silver bullet. Inevitably, I and others at Saturn smile when someone comes and they ask questions. They may not exactly say, "Tell me what the silver bullet is," but in so many words that's really what they're asking. What makes Saturn successful is the sum of many, many pieces, and there are many layers to those pieces. Maybe I'm too close to it and someone from the outside might say, "You're in too deep and you just love it too much, and you see all these subtleties and nuances but they're not all important." But I really have a perception, after being away from Saturn for three years (from 1992 to 1995), that there is no silver bullet. There's no easy thing that comes in and kind of grabs hold, and it's not even as simple as the culture. The culture has developed lots of more hard business strategies and processes that are very hard to duplicate, from service to much more technical things. Like how we do service engineering, how we do parts, how we move parts around the country, and how we get information through computers on what happened on the cars in our service facilities yesterday. All of those things have now grown up over a period of time and have a foundation that's not just culture. But as I said there's one part here—the systems and processes that make up a pretty powerful part—and it goes through lots of different pieces of the business. Like the fact that we structure our distribution around a market area franchise and not point-by-point like other auto manufacturers. All of these things that are not cultural, they're kind of hard strategic direction. They too are also very, very hard to duplicate for somebody who is not a new entrant.

Question: Many people say that Saturn goofed by not coming out with a larger car sooner. What was the reasoning, and how has this affected customer loyalty?

Answer: Virtually every person at General Motors and Saturn would say, "Gosh, we would have loved to have come out with a larger car sooner." Knowing what we know today, we would have loved to be out with a larger car already, so why not? To have had a car on the road in 1997 means that—given lead times, etc., in this business, which are at times frustratingly long—a decision would have had to been made in 1992 or maybe early 1993. What everybody forgets, now that it's mid-1998, is that General Motors—who among other things was basically our banker and sole source of financial support—was teetering on the verge of bankruptcy in late 1992 and early 1993. GM was trying to figure out how to come up with enough funds to continue to make car loans through GMAC, and was selling assets to continue to fund car brand product development that had been planned for years. That's just a long-winded way of saying that it was a really bad time in '92 and '93 to try and bet another huge chunk of money behind Saturn. In 20/20 hindsight, everybody certainly wished it would have been done, but at the time the decision would have had to been made, it would have been a very, very, very difficult thing for GM to do. The net consequence of that is we'll have a midsize car next year, and further product-line growth beyond that. But for 1997 and 1998, we've got the products that we've got.

How has this affected customer loyalty? I shared with you earlier that approximately half of the customers who buy a small sporty car buy some other segment of car the next time around, and undoubtedly not having a larger car is apparently why we lose that roughly half of the people. I think some of those people are holding on to their cars a while longer, waiting for Saturn to have a midsize car, and some have immediate needs that say they have to get a larger car, and hopefully they'll circle back to Saturn at some point down the road. So it has had an impact on loyalty. But despite the fact that everybody wishes we had a midsize car a year ago, I don't think—if we were to fast-forward this conversation to 5 years from now or 10 years from now—that anybody will find it worth writing that Saturn launched a larger car in '99 versus '98 versus '97.

Question: Saturn had the advantage of doing this with a "clean-paper" approach. How realistic is it to expect old, well-established companies to make the necessary changes?

Answer: Much of what I've already said really addresses this. Doing what we did, we made the most of the clean-paper approach that we were given. Now with that said, there's a bunch of disadvantages to clean paper. There's a lot more opportunities to do things wrong, and it's an expensive approach, to be honest. Nonetheless, we believe that with strong commitment, the lessons of Saturn need not only apply to those who have a clean-sheet-of-paper approach.

My favorite story actually is not of Saturn in the United States in this regard, but of Saturn in Canada. Unlike in the United States, Saturn in Canada did not start with a clean sheet of retailers. There was a network that GM of Canada was running, called "Passport." The reason it was called Passport is GM of Canada sort of bundled all the cars imported from the Middle East and from Europe under this "passport" umbrella and it was their import channel. The Passport channel never performed very well. As a result, the retail facilities were never that great. No one would have accused Passport of being a leading-edge, top-quality retail service organization. The strategy we collectively took with our partners at GM in Canada was not to start from scratch, but in fact to completely reconfigure this network that had been called Passport, and establish a new network (which is now called Saturn-Saab-Isuzu). The network that sells Saturns in Canada also sells Saabs and Isuzus, although Saturns are the vast majority of the sales. The performance generated in Canada on the first day we started selling there, which goes back to late 1991, was not as good as the U.S. performance on their first day. But the Saturn-Saab-Isuzu management worked very closely with their U.S. counterparts and accessed the training and all of the strategic thinking. They have, over the course of the years, established Saturn-Saab-Isuzu as the leader in customer enthusiasm in all automotive retailing in Canada. They worked systematically on training; they worked systematically to restructure the distribution network; they put in place market area approach instead of single-point franchising; they refurbished facilities and in many cases relocated them and started from scratch. Again, they didn't have our customer enthusiasm success from the first day. But through a steady, applied effort using the principles of both the hard stuff (the strategies, the processes, the systems), as well as the cultural focus (the values, the philosophy), they have in fact achieved a position in the Canadian market that is similar to Saturn's position in the United States for our retail market. The lesson from that? I would say it's not impossible to take a established situation and "Saturnize it," but it does take some time and it takes discipline and dedication to do it. But the reward ultimately is there.

Question: How does Saturn meet the challenge of continuing to create customer loyalty?

Answer: That's a pretty good summary of my job description! There's certainly no one part of that, and perhaps the greatest, most important part is no complacency whatsoever. It's really interesting, when I was away from Saturn for three years, from a distance I continued to be just so impressed with Saturn. I almost got more impressed with Saturn the more time I spent away. When I came back, I was really struck by the *paranoia* (the word that came to mind at the time) within Saturn about maintaining its leadership. And it really resonated with me when Andy Grove came out with his book a couple years ago, called *Only the Paranoid Survive.* I hope that Saturn always remains paranoid about maintaining a leadership in customer enthusiasm. I know complacency is enormously dangerous. We do work hard to establish systems and measures. Obviously we have all sorts of systems and measures and, quite honestly, we would never say that they tell us that we do a great job every time. In fact, I use the quote, "I think we hit the ball out of the park with customers maybe four times out of five, and our single greatest opportunity is not reinventing our approach to our customer service, but hitting the ball out of the park five out of five times." I don't think we drop the ball in that one case out of five, but we might not hit it out of the park. So, consistency—the 100 percent kind of consistency—is no different really from building the car on process to spec 100 percent of the time. Consistency in our service is our greatest opportunity. At the same time, we do work pretty hard to establish and try to identify benchmark situations—companies that we can learn from. We have never felt that auto retailing itself is much of a benchmark, so we've always studied others. In the earliest days we studied Nordstrom and Southwest Airlines. We have studied and worked with Disney quite a bit, and we continue to look for those situations—anywhere in the world, in any industry, in any category of retailing or service—where we have a sense that people are doing things well, and we want to go out there and learn from them. So that gives you some sense of what our focus is there. The keys seem to be that paranoia is a lot better than complacency; that consistency is our number one opportunity; and that benchmarking the best service wherever it might be gives us a guidepost in terms of lessons to be learned and captured.

CHAPTER

12

Get Saturnized!

THE SATURN WAY OF DOING BUSINESS AND CREATING CUSTOMER loyalty is not perfect, but what is? In the words of one new Saturn customer, "With Saturn, I think I've seen about 2 horror stories, and 300 people saying it's great, so that puts it into perspective." Keep your perspective, and keep your focus on creating loyal customers by treating people right.

"I've been Saturnized!"

There is one noticeable "difference" about Saturn customer Charlie Brown. It's the Saturn logo tattoo on his leg! Let me tell you the story behind Charlie's tattoo.

Charlie started doing his research on Saturn cars in November 1991, then made his first Saturn purchase—a 1992 blue-green SL2 (four-door sedan). He was pleased with the way he was treated at the dealership. According to Charlie, "The main thing that impressed me was their no-hassle sales approach." Then one day in 1993, Charlie took his car to a Saturn dealership in Columbus, Ohio, for its 38,000-mile service. He wasn't thinking of buying or selling, but when he discovered that his SL2's trade-in value was only $700 less than what he had paid for the car two years previously, he couldn't resist. A 1994 plum-colored Saturn wagon joined Charlie's family.

When Saturn Corporation invited all Saturn owners and their families to the Homecoming at the plant in Spring Hill, Tennessee, in 1994, Charlie was there along with 44,000 other Saturn fans. One of the activities that Charlie participated in that weekend was getting a "Homecoming 1994 Saturn logo" tattoo—the wash-off kind. Charlie is no teenager; I won't reveal his exact age except to say that he's well over 40. Well, Charlie reasoned that Harley-Davidson motorcycle owners get tattoos. Charlie didn't own a motorcycle, but he owned a Saturn. So, he decided to make the tattoo permanent, and in Charlie's words, he "got Saturnized."

Today, a couple of Saturn cars later, Charlie now serves as president of the Nature Coast Saturn CarClub in Florida. And, he still has his tattoo.

It's not necessary to tattoo everybody in the company to "get Saturnized." Instead, I leave you with a painless way to help remember how to treat customers—before, during, and after the purchase. It's my acronym for SATURN. Put it into practice, and you're on the road to getting Saturnized.

- S - SEEK to create interest by building a reputation through quality, through your loyal customers, and by being different.

- A - ACKNOWLEDGE customers when they contact you, and help them feel welcome by applying the Golden Rules.

- T - TREAT customers to a hassle-free and easy buying experience.

- U - UP your opportunities for success with follow-UP and communication after the sale.

R - RECOGNIZE problems as opportunities to create loyal customers, and go the extra mile to prevent and solve problems.

N - NEVER forget to show your appreciation, and always give customers reasons to keep coming back.

Our point is this: In today's competitive market it's important to have a really great product, and we're very pleased that we do. But, what's equally important is the extra effort we make to create an ownership experience that's comfortable and trusting for our customers.

Beyond all the smart technological features built into our cars, this is the real difference that we bring to the table—a willingness to make the right gestures so that owning a Saturn feels more like a friendship, not just a business transaction.

From the Saturn Owner's Handbook

Notes

Chapter 2
1. Remarks by Roger B. Smith, chairman, General Motors Corporation, at the Saturn news conference, GM Technical Center, Warren, Michigan; from company news release dated January 8, 1985.

Chapter 3
2. *The Loyalty Effect*, Frederick F. Reichheld, Bain & Company, Inc., Harvard Business School Press, Boston, 1996, pp. 36–37.
3. *Customers for Life*, Carl Sewell and Paul B. Brown, Pocket Books, New York, 1990.
4. *The Pursuit of WOW!*, Tom Peters, Vintage Books, New York, 1994, p. 189.

Chapter 4
5. Stephen Covey, as quoted in the 1997-1998 Catalog of Training Services, Saturn Consulting Services, Saturn Corporation, 1997. Covey is the author of *The 7 Habits of Highly Effective People*, A Fireside Book, Simon & Schuster, New York, 1989.

Chapter 5

6. *The Loyalty Effect,* Frederick F. Reichheld, Bain & Company, Inc., Harvard Business School Press, Boston, 1996, p. 3.

7. "Real people drive Saturn ads to popularity," article from *USA Today* web page, November 3, 1997.

Chapter 9

8. "Click and Clak Talk Cars," article by Tom and Ray Magliozzi, King Features, New York, November 8, 1996.

Chapter 10

9. "Toyota tactics drive some buyers away," article by Donald W. Nauss in the *Los Angeles Times,* reprinted in *The Louisville Courier-Journal,* September 23, 1997.

Chapter 11

10. Vicki Lenz interview with Joe Kennedy, May 29, 1998.

Index

Resale value, 77, 78
Respect, 55–58, 118
Retailers, 15
    compensation from, 47
    "market area approach," 53
Retention, value of customer, 28
    (*See also* Loyalty, customer)
Returning customers,
    how to make, 213–214
Reviewing internal procedures, 149–150
Rewards, 203
Right-to-Know training, 58
Risk & Reward program, 45–46
    service suppliers on, 53
Road & Track magazine, 69
Roadside assistance, 198
Rosenblum, Dave, 54

Saab, 259
Safety, 75–78
Sales:
    consultants, 127, 132–133
    consultative process of, 143–146
    importance of speed in, 144
    interviewing part of, 144–146
    no-hassle, no-haggle, 125–126
    people in, 239–242
    Saturn's process of, 127–128
Sales calls, 29
Sales Satisfaction Index, 4
SATURN, the acronym, 264–265
Saturnalia, 225–229
Saturn Car Care, 152
Saturn Consulting Services, 60
Saturn Corporation:
    accessories, 97
    awards and milestones of, 17–23
    birth of, 11–14
    brochures, 137, 139
    of Canada, 259–260
    "clean-sheet-of-paper" approach of,
        12, 24, 36, 258–260
    commercials, 86–90
    communications team, 59
    community involvement of, 54–55
    core values in, 42
    culture of, 61
    customer update form of, 240
    definition of, 31
    design studio of, 71

"difference" of, 14–16, 24
employee evaluations in, 56–57
environmental concerns of, 14, 71
first car of, 14
focus groups of, 234–235
follow-up communication from,
    162–164
gifts from, 184–187
guarantee, 138, 140
Homecoming, 215–218, 244, 264
in Japan, 244–245
mail policy of, 172
mission of, 33
name of, 11
philosophy of, 34
retailers, 15–16
sales consultants, 127, 132–133
send-off, 156–157
success of, 16
toll-free phone number of, 107
used cars of, 139–141
web site of, 98–99, 136, 182–183
Saturn Customer Communications
    (SCC), 164, 239
Saturn New Owner Workshops, 167–168
Saturn of Louisville, 96–97, 113–114,
    132–133, 178–180
Saturn Playgrounds, 55
Saturn SL2, 77
Saturn University, 60
Seminars (*see* Workshops)
Service records, 237–238
Servicing, automobile:
    departments, 16
    questionnaires about, 175–176
    reliability of Saturn's, 195–196
*The Seven Habits of Highly Effective
    People,* 58
Sewell, Carl, 28
Showrooms, appearance of, 119–121
Sign language, 51
Sincerity, importance of, 187, 224
Skillets, 57
Smile, importance of, 117
Smith, Roger B., 12, 14
Soybeans, 48
Space race, 11
Spring Hill, Tennessee, 14
    employee orientation at, 130–131
    Homecoming event at, 215–218